THE
FRAMEWORK LIFE

Three Pillars of Success

Change Is Coming

John D. Inscoe

FRAMEWORK MEDIA GROUP

Washington, D.C.

THREE PILLARS OF SUCCESS

Copyright © 2020 by John D. Inscoe

Framework Media Group, LLC.

www.frameworklife.com

THE
FRAMEW◉RK LIFE

Cover Design by Rossitsa Atanassova

Selected graphic elements licensed from 123RF.com

ISBN-13: 978-1-946562-00-5

Printed in the United States of America

PREFACE

I chose the subtitle of the book, *"Change is Coming,"* for two reasons:

1. The world around us changes, without giving notice or asking permission.
2. We can achieve the successes we want by creating the changes we need, and without giving notice or asking permission either.

We just need a little help. So, the statement *"Change Is Coming"* is both a warning and a call to action. Change will always happen around us, but we can win the battle for success by thinking about, planning for, and taking the right actions to achieve that success.

Welcome to *The Framework Life*, the project I created to help people **transform** their lives and create levels of success they never knew could be theirs. You and I haven't met, but I understand how hard that's been. We're all human, and we've all been limited by the same challenges in the past. But we can change that now, by learning a bit about our own psychology and how it affects our ability to succeed. We can change *who we are* to achieve *what we've always wanted*, and we can do it starting today.

Three Pillars of Success was written with you in mind, and to help you make those changes. It's a standardized and repeatable system, and it represents everything I've learned about success in the last 35 years. It's also the passion that drives everything I do.

At the age of 49 I left my IT career to start doing what I'm sharing with you here, because I realized my *"successful life"* wasn't actually successful at all. I was making $325,000 a year at the time, with plenty of money in the bank, a nice house, and all the *"things"* I thought I needed. What I discovered was that I didn't have real satisfaction. I realized that *things* never made me feel successful, and the idea of working for 15 more years until retirement felt like a prison sentence.

I couldn't *"see myself"* continuing to live that way, so I stopped what I was doing, redesigned my life, and changed everything. You see, my generation was raised to believe that money would make us successful. We were also told to work hard and wait for our turn. However, without knowing how to earn more money, and having the skills to deal with change, we struggled and felt like failures.

And all that struggle is happening right now, to more people than ever before. Everyone is waiting for their turn, without knowing how to design the successful life they want. That's why our lives are where they are today, because we've been taught that success is a destination we *"get to"* versus a lifestyle, a state of mind, and a *Journey* we create.

Success comes from teaching yourself to become a *Successful Person*, which is why I say this:

Change *is* coming,
and—starting today—it begins with you.

INTRODUCTION

We've been misled about money, education, and success our whole lives, and we've done all the wrong things because of it. I should say we didn't do enough of the *right things*, which is actually the bigger problem. We went to school, got educated, got jobs and careers and worked hard like we were told to, but it wasn't enough. We also followed the rules handed to us by our parents, teachers, and everyone we knew.

But ask yourself this:

> ## Where did following the rules take us,
> ## and did we get everything we wanted?

For most of us the answer is "***not where we thought***," and "***not even close.***" We didn't find the success we wanted, or hoped would result from doing all the things we were told to believe in.

Following the rules didn't create the life I wanted, so I took my 21 years of experience with successful IT projects and turned that into a system that *will*. In my lifelong journey to understand success, I discovered three foundational areas we need to change.

I call them *Three Pillars of Success*, and I've created a three-step process to help you leverage them:

Step 1: Redefine what success means.

Step 2: Become the *type of person* who can achieve that success.

Step 3: Turn off your fears, uncertainties, and doubts so you can take action and succeed.

Throughout the book I'm going to *prove* how simple this is, and how it will work for you. I'm also going to prove my next statement, so it will stop being an obstacle between you and the success you've been missing:

> ## Money does not (and never <u>will</u>) make you successful.

To some that might sound crazy, because it seems like every successful person has a ton of it; but there's much more to the story. Money is a tool that can help us achieve our goals, but by itself doesn't measure success.

In fact, money doesn't measure any of the qualities that successful people have, like ***passion, skill,*** and the ***ability to overcome challenges***.

All that money measures is the collection of currency, which is great to have, but isn't a substitute for succeeding at something you worked hard for. So, before we go further, you should test my statement about money by answering this:

What do you call someone who wins the lottery?

Is that person Successful? Or just Lucky?

We reserve the title of *Successful* for people with *accomplishments* we *admire* and *respect*. Professional athletes, musicians, and Hollywood stars are examples of that, and what we're drawn to is their hard work, talent, and achievements. Money isn't why we love them, it's just the reward, or we could say byproduct, of what they've done.

To change our lives now, we have to think about money that way too, and the first step is to see there are two types of successes: *Personal* and *Financial.*

To make the most money we have to start with bigger and better personal achievements. I call those **Great Accomplishments**, because when we reach them, they make us feel like nothing else can. They can be designed to create wealth, and maximizing our income requires we have them, but money is not what makes them great. Instead, they motivate us to keep improving our skills and accomplishments, in all areas of our lives, when we achieve them.

That's what real success is.

Nelson Mandela achieved his greatest accomplishments while in prison. He served 27 years of a life sentence before being released, and never gave up on what he believed in. He also never thought he had failed and kept working with political opposition leaders on the outside to help end Apartheid. His efforts transformed South Africa into a democracy for all races, and in 1994 Mandela made history as South Africa's first black president.

He was guided by great accomplishments, and history will remember him as a great success, but money had nothing to do with it. Mandela was driven by a never-ending passion to bring equality to all South Africans, and successful is the only way you could describe his life.

That's The Secret: Great accomplishments are the building blocks we need, because being successful means achieving our goals at the highest levels we can. Then we go further, by improving our skills to reach for the *next* highest level of accomplishment. Without that approach, we're working backward, trying to feel successful by making money in jobs and careers we don't care about. Then, without anything great to reward us, the money becomes disappointing and we feel incomplete no matter how fat our bank accounts become.

That's why millions of people work in *"some job,"* at *"some company,"* doing things that don't motivate or fulfill them. They started working for the money above anything else, hoping that feelings of success would follow. They hoped that (somehow) they would begin to enjoy themselves, but it never happened. Then, without the proper skills to get the right jobs later, they got stuck where they were and felt like failures.

However, when we know what makes us feel the most accomplished, and have goals which only focus on achieving that, we'll be able to get the right jobs to support our journey to greater success.

The reality is we're on our own when it comes to building a career. Maximizing our skills to create great accomplishments is the only way to control the outcome, and that begins with developing the skills we love to use. Then we apply those skills in career positions that pay us the most. That's how to feel our most accomplished and get paid the most for our efforts.

Compared to taking a job for the money and hoping things "*work out*," designing our careers with a purpose is what we need to be doing.

During that process, if you find the jobs you need don't exist, it might be the signal to create your own business (or even a new industry) for doing what you love. *The Framework Life* was started that way, because—after 21 years in Information Technology—I needed great accomplishments that no job could offer.

I left that life behind once I discovered my passion did not lie in technology, but instead was writing about and mentoring others for success. And once I got started, I worked six or seven days a week on my goals. When you're driven by a passion like that, it's easy, and doesn't feel like work. Having great accomplishments as the focus of your goals is what you need to create that passion.

Creating Your Reality: If you can invent something new, improve something old, or even be the best worker in your field, you'll figure out your great accomplishments. That's also how to earn the most money you can and build the career you want with purpose. A new job or a new company might have the opportunities you want, or as I said you might need to start your own business or industry to create them.

It's the same route professional athletes have followed since childhood. After mastering one set of skills, they joined another team that could take them to the next higher level. They always knew where they were going, because becoming a pro was the first great accomplishment on their list.

They did it; I did it; and now it's your turn.

By now you can see we've been using the wrong definition of success for a long time and chasing after money without the right skills to earn "*a lot of it.*" That's not what success is about, but you probably know people who are struggling this way, in the hope that things will change "*someday.*"

Too many people are unhappy with their lives, and don't know how to change because they're not even sure it can be done. But it can and starting today we can shift our focus toward achieving great accomplishments to create that change. That's what *Three Pillars of Success* was designed for, to help people transform from the old version of themselves to the new.

Helping people do that is my passion, and it feels like a great accomplishment every time I do. I left an established career to follow that passion, and my job now is to show you how to find and follow yours. When you're not in the wrong job, and focused only on making money, you can think more clearly about the life you really want to create.

Earlier, I said I was going to prove how this is all possible, which is another part of my job. But you have a job as well, which you've already started by reading this far. The next step is to believe you can do this and keep reading so I can show you how.

It's not that you're certain about everything right now, but that you're ready for a change like I was. Having that fire inside is the key for transforming yourself, and we all need a little help to get started.

This is the place for that help, and this is the time for that change.

Are you ready?

Let's begin...

CHAPTER 1

We Were Born to Succeed.

Now that we know the truth about great accomplishments being the secret to our success, let's talk about why they've been so hard to create.

The Problem with Success: Our problem started so long ago we don't even know that it happened. It affected the skills we developed, the jobs we took, and the income we earned our whole life. And the entire time it felt completely normal, so none of us knew there was a problem.

When you don't know something is missing, you know you don't go looking for it, and you also don't think about better choices when you don't even know they exist. But they've always existed, and they've always been yours to go after.

Believe me, I know the chapter title is pretty bold and you might have some doubts, but it's absolutely true. We were all born to succeed; it's just that something changed the path we were on long ago. To fix that, we need to understand how the change happened, and how it led to the series of events that brought us to where we are right now.

Understanding that will give us a power we haven't had before, and help in two ways:

1. We won't make the same mistakes again.
2. We'll feel in control of our lives, starting now, and into the future.

Where It All Began: As little kids we were success machines. We were constantly in motion to explore our world, overcome challenges, and become the most accomplished we could at the things we loved doing. Back then it was easy, because there was a fire inside us that drove our thoughts and actions toward succeeding.

Then we got older, and people started to say our fire got in the way. Parents and teachers said that it was disruptive, because—until recently—not even Psychologists understood that "*play time,*" and "*being a kid*" were the building blocks we needed most for human development and success. Whatever its intentions might have been, school taught us to hold ourselves back, and conform to the rules of the classroom.

Starting in pre-school or kindergarten, success became defined as this:

> *Being quiet. Being obedient. Doing our schoolwork in the way we were told.*

Even in college, success was measured by **how well we suppressed our ability to succeed** and did what we were told instead. That's how we became conditioned for limited accomplishments outside of school, and where our problem with succeeding began.

Because school focused on academics, the life and work skills we would need as adults weren't taught. Things like critical thinking, problem solving, and the psychology of working with others are what we needed but didn't get. We were told to focus on schoolwork instead, to get promoted to the next grade level, and worry about the real world "*later.*"

From the 1950s through the 1990s we managed to get by with that type of ignorance, but the world became a very different place by the turn of the new millennium. To be successful now, and maximize our accomplishments and income, we must change the way we think and act.

Example: The *right* job in the *right* industry builds the *right* career.

Imagine you're a new college graduate, and you hear about a job opportunity from someone you know. You submit your resume, do well in the interviews, and the company makes you an offer. It seems like a reasonable course of action, doesn't it? After all, you need to earn money and you've always been told that you have to "*start somewhere.*"

But if you "*start somewhere*" just to get some cash, how does that lead you to the right job in the right industry to create the right career? How can you achieve the life you want by starting off randomly, with no real plan in mind?

The short answer is that you can't, because random choices lead to random results. If you want specific results, you have to make specific choices that are designed to bring them to you.

Too often, our careers get formed by the first jobs we choose and the industries we settle into. We find ourselves on paths that we haven't consciously chosen, and we follow them for the rest of our lives without realizing that we've eliminated some choices for the future.

That's why we need to think about and design our changes carefully. It's the most powerful skill for creating success, and it's always free to do. Throughout this book I'll remind you that thinking and designing are free, compared to taking actions which can cost us time, money, and other resources. Like Nelson Mandela, we should think and design carefully, using what we have at that moment to get our best results. That way, when things change unexpectedly, we'll be able to change more quickly to fix the problem and keep progressing toward success.

So many people have jobs and careers they don't like because they feel like change isn't possible. They've never known how to do it, and without some help they feel stuck. That's when we fall back on the emotions of *hoping, wishing, and wondering* if things will "*someday work out.*"

But hoping, wishing, and wondering aren't skills, and we can't practice them to create results. Instead, we're going to use some tools and techniques that teach us to build the skills we need to drive the changes we want.

It's true we can't plan for everything ahead of time, and I'm not suggesting that we can. But we can build a foundation of skills that make us ready and better-able to deal with change. We can learn to recover from setbacks and failures more easily, so we can revise our plans to keep moving forward.

Our lives are not limited because we did something wrong, or there's something wrong with us, we just had the wrong recipe for how to create success.

That's what *Three Pillars of Success* was created to fix:

    Pillar 1 - A new definition of success, with the right recipe to get us there.

    Pillar 2 - Techniques to change our Personal Identity and become the *type of person* who can achieve that success.

    Pillar 3 - Identifying the Fears, Uncertainties, and Doubts that keep us from changing ourselves, and turning them into tools we can use to succeed.

We can create our greatest successes when we know how. I'm going to help you do it in bigger ways and at faster speeds than ever before. It's not as hard as you think, and there's no reason you should wait any longer.

And in case that sounds like marketing, let me say it a different way:

I'm going to prove we are able, and entitled, to make these changes today.

When I say entitled, I don't mean the world owes us something. Instead, we are free-thinking people who have the right to design the life we want. We are *entitled* to transform ourselves by planning better, and changing faster, and we don't have to wait for "*later*," or "*someday*."

The concepts I've created here are based in human psychology, because knowing more about why we think and act the way we do will help us transform more quickly.

My journey to learn these lessons taught me two important things:

1. Success doesn't happen to you; it happens *through you*.

2. Success is not reserved for "*Other People*."

A young woman I know told me that she couldn't believe succeeding was so simple, because it always seemed complex and out of her reach in the past. So, don't get frustrated if it feels that way for you too, and for now keep reading so you can prove to yourself how simple it is.

We live at an amazing time in history, where information is everywhere, and your skills are what stand between you and greater success. When you have clear goals, with the skills to create those accomplishments, success no longer feels like work. It actually becomes a natural extension of you the more you do it, and your entire life changes with the right recipe to guide you.

So, as you're reading the next few chapters, think about this question:

Who do I want to become today?

CHAPTER 2

Our Three Pillars of Success

Pillar 1 - The Recipe for Success.

Pillar 2 - Personal Identity - Who Am I, and What Can I Do?

Pillar 3 - F.U.D. - Our Fears, Uncertainties, and Doubts.

Some authors will say that success comes from thinking positively, making lists, or visualizing the life you want. I agree those are tools we can use, but without understanding why they work, and the other things we need to transform our lives, our Recipe for Success isn't complete.

So, I created *Three Pillars* to give us what we need to create the life we want.

I know that might sound simplistic, but for now keep an open mind that transforming our lives could be easier than we know. In fact, until we prove to ourselves what our skills, abilities, and limits add up to, we have no way of knowing what we can achieve. To begin, the levels of success we have today, in all parts of our lives, were created from those three things. By improving our skills and abilities, and minimizing the factors that limit us, our levels of success will always be able to grow.

How Three Pillars Affect Us: When our pillars are equal in strength and size, they support our goals like a stool supports our weight. On a stool, each leg does an equal amount of the work to provide a strong and balanced platform.

You could say our pillars support the *"weight"* of our goals, and just like a stool the amount of support they can provide depends on ***how we build the legs***.

That's not meant as a catchy phrase; that's how this works. Based on the strength and balance of our pillars, we're driven to act in one of three ways:

1. Set challenging goals to achieve more than we did before.

2. Set easier goals and convince ourselves that's good enough.

3. Take a pause, and don't think about goals at all.

That's how powerful the pillars are for creating positive or negative results. And because we didn't know they existed we didn't know how much they were affecting us. That's why it can feel like life is *"happening to us,"* and we don't have any control. But we can change that today by understanding that the pillars exist, what they do, and how they do it.

Without understanding them, the pillars follow a "Cycle of Limits" that reinforces itself and says we can't do any better. Until someone, or something interrupts that pattern, we simply won't.

The cycle works backward from Pillar to 3 to 1:

- It starts with our fears, uncertainties, and doubts, which we call F.U.D., telling us to avoid the things we fear and don't understand.

- F.U.D. then influences our Personal Identity (P.I.), which is Pillar 2. P.I. tells us the *type of person* we are, and the *kinds of goals* we can accomplish. F.U.D. says each type of person can only do certain things, which is how we hit mental boundaries that limit what we think we can achieve.

- Limited goals mean we create limited successes. That reinforces our belief in the wrong Recipe for Success, which says it's defined by having "*a lot of money*" that we aren't good enough to earn.

As an example, we sometimes ask ourselves why we're not accomplishing more, or challenging ourselves. Sometimes a family member or a friend asks that, and F.U.D. steps in to protect us from change by reminding us that we're "*not that type of person.*" It says we're okay to be right where we are, because we're not smarter, more athletic, or more ambitious, to name a few. What we have is just fine, and F.U.D. reminds us that we don't want to be asked again.

That's how easily our Cycle of Limits gets reinforced, because—without knowing that it exists—we don't even realize it's happening to us. As crazy as it may sound, every goal we ever set was affected this way without us knowing. So, with few exceptions, everything we've accomplished in the past was limited by these psychological forces we never heard of.

As mentioned earlier, this cycle started when we were little kids, so by now it feels like our normal decision-making process. We don't think anything is out of place, and we're pretty sure we know "*who we are.*"

That's the reason we stop trying to do more, every time.

Until we know how to change ourselves into a different *type of person*, we will never believe we can transform our life. But we can, and I'll show you how our Cycle of Limits can become a Cycle of Success instead.

That happens when achieving greater levels of success at a faster speed becomes our new decision-making process. You might not believe it's so simple, but you can do this by changing how your pillars are built to support you.

Until you learn how they work, and how to change them to work for you, it's hard to imagine *who you could become*, and *what you could accomplish*. Our past performances make us think our futures will be more of the same, because that's what they've always been.

And without a better recipe to guide us, what would change our mind?

One simple question will help: **How do I know?**

How do I *know* this doesn't work, won't work for me, or won't work this time?

Every professional athlete, musician, and Hollywood star asked themselves these questions once, and now it's our turn. Even though we think those people were "*born to be the best*," they had to do the same things I'm offering to you here.

If they never changed their pillars, to become who we know them as today, they would simply be the most talented people *we've never heard of.*

Our lives weren't created by fate, karma, or destiny.
It was always Three Pillars of Success.

CHAPTER 3

Pillar 1 - The Recipe for Success

Success is a vague and frustrating concept because it doesn't have a standard measurement we can agree on, like grams, or degrees, or miles. In the absence of an objective standard for success, people often default to what seems like the obvious choice; Money.

But obvious doesn't mean proven, and we talked about how our personal and financial successes only come from achieving great accomplishments.

In this chapter, we're going to talk about the recipe for success we should be using, why the one from our past didn't work, and how the right one is needed to design the future we want.

To make it easier to follow, I've divided the chapter into three sections:

1. How we learned about success.

2. Changing the definition of success to work for us.

3. How to succeed with accomplishments, goals, and actions that we ***prove***.

Section 1 - How We Learned About Success.

When I was a kid in the 1970's, the idea of success was simple. Whenever someone had a better life than we did, with a nicer home, bigger income, and a fancy car we saw them as "*Successful.*" Success meant having nicer things than others did, and nicer things were more expensive, so it seemed logical that having more money must be the definition of a successful life.

My peers had those ideas too, because we all had relatives who lived through the Great Depression and World War II, when money was scarce. Our elders defined success as making as much money as you could, though they never dreamed of making millions. Their vision of success was about avoiding risk and creating *safety*.

That's how you "*successfully*" provided for a family back then, and financial safety is really what the "*American Dream*" was all about. Those ideals reinforced how safety was the real definition of succeeding for "*normal people,*" who never expected to make "*a lot of money.*"

To create that safety, everyone said you needed three things:

1. A Stable Job.

2. Benefits.

3. A Pension for Retirement.

Every family we knew thought the same way, and my friends and I ended up adopting financial security as our definition of success. But success also had limits according to our relatives, and they said things like "*a stable job is all you can hope for.*"

They believed once you got one you stayed there forever and didn't expect more. In the era before personal (and portable) retirement options, like 401k accounts and IRAs, people kept their jobs for 30 or 40 years to qualify for a pension.

That made them like indentured servants and created the cultural belief that it was necessary to accept whatever your employer gave you, because "*that's just how it works.*" Many of my relatives had faced poverty, hunger, and homelessness in the past, so they put up with whatever they had to for the promise of stability.

The economy had changed dramatically by the time I was in grade school, but my parents' generation didn't understand—or even recognize—the change. As a result, the lessons they taught us about life, career choices, and finances were hopelessly out of date. In my experience, that's how safety became the unspoken substitute for real success in so many families. And though it was 40 years ago when I learned those lessons, *not much has changed.*

Parents and educators have been teaching those same outdated lessons since I was a kid, and they're doing it to the next group of kids as we speak. Those ideas were started in the 1950's, but people don't realize how outmoded and disempowering they are because they've been around so long.

We've all adopted those ideas as enduring wisdom, when they're nearly the exact opposite.

This process of passing on the same flawed lessons you learned growing up is so dangerous that some Psychologists study it their whole careers. It's called the *Illusory Truth Effect*, and it means that things seem more believable when we hear them repeated often, and from a diverse group of people. Think about ads you've watched or heard on TV, radio, and YouTube. At some point after the fourth (or fourteenth) time, they start to seem legitimate. They begin to seem *true*, even if we're completely aware that the content is nothing more than marketing.

And when the message you hear from your family for the 13 - 17 years you're in school says, "*get educated and get a safe job*," it's easy to accept.

But this phenomenon is called illusory for a reason. It only *appears* to be real, because we're exposed to it so often and so thoroughly. We've been working with bad information we learned from an outdated system of beliefs and acting like things are the way they're supposed to be.

It's no wonder that being accomplished and successful feels so damn hard.

When I went to college in 1986, we could only follow our passion if it led to the kind of stable job our parents thought of as normal and safe. If not, we were taking an unacceptable risk, and we were told to make better (i.e., safer) choices. Looking back, it's easy to see how so many of us have known less, done less, and gotten less from our efforts because of those faulty lessons that we accepted as true.

The Illusory Truth was reinforced again, and again, and again, so by the time we left college we knew that all we could hope for was a job, benefits, and a retirement plan.

By the 1990's things were changing; the economy had changed, and the internet had transformed communications in a way we had never seen. Unfortunately, we were still following the rules for life that were decades behind reality. The world was a different place, but no one told us that we could (and should) become different too.

It seems like most of us grew up thinking life was supposed to be difficult, with obstacles we couldn't overcome. We didn't know exactly what they might be, or how we were supposed to deal with them, but everyone made sure we knew to be afraid of them.

My family said things like:

> *"Don't do too much."*

> *"Don't expect so much."* and

> *"Don't be disappointed if things don't work out."*

It was generic language I call *"Failure Talk,"* because it's based in ignorance and fear that keeps us from succeeding. But my teachers and family didn't have better lessons to give, so I got what they had to offer.

That's not their fault, but it is how we got set up for failure by the Illusory Truth. And when we don't have people or information to guide us in a better way, it's easy to settle down with what we have and what we think is true.

But it's 2020 now, and you would think my experience comes from a time in history that's done and gone. At this point you might be wondering why any of this matters now, or to you. But it does, because as I write this people of all ages are failing from the same limitations I just shared, **and they don't know what to do about it**.

The lessons I learned in the 1970's were created in the 1950's, and they're still being handed down today without people knowing how they create a culture of fear and failure. And that's not meant as an insult, it's simply the report card that shows us what's been happening and why. We keep believing in our childhood lessons because we don't have better information, and we don't know to go look for it.

That's why we need a new recipe for success, to empower us to redesign the goals we failed at, didn't succeed enough in, or are struggling to finish. Once we identify our outdated and limiting beliefs, we can stop using them and move on to the right ones.

When I was researching how money, safety, and success got turned into this single, vague concept I realized these old-school fears and failures are the reason so many Millennials are unhappy. They don't know who they are, what they're capable of, or how they could live the lives people say they should be. So, it's unfair and unrealistic when people criticize them, as though they're just being rebellious and not following the rules.

It's the rules that created the problem, and it's the rules we need to change.

Like any of us, Millennials are doing what they can to survive after growing up with the wrong training and the wrong leadership. I believe they're the first generation to receive the outdated lessons of the 20th century without having an economy they can use them in. They got the same *"get to safety"* training that I did 40 years ago and were expected to somehow *"find success."*

But the idea of school leading to jobs, money, and success no longer works like it once did. Money still creates safety, but it's harder to get than before. And without tying it to goals that make us feel greatly accomplished, it's really not so valuable.

This scenario of limited accomplishments and unsuccessful lessons is the same, no matter your age. I mentioned Millennials to show the immediate danger their generation is in, but they are not alone.

The problem of old-school rules keeping us safe, *but not successful*, affects everyone. We know this because a Gallup poll conducted in 2017 found that over 75% of people in the U.S. hate their jobs.

Think about that. Three out of four people in the American work force hate the jobs they go to every day. These people are doing the minimum to get by, because they have no great accomplishments to inspire them, and no idea they can change their lives to create some.

That's called surviving, not succeeding, and thankfully we can do something about it in section two.

Section 2 - Changing the Definition of Success to Work for Us.

To change how we plan for and achieve success we need to start with a better definition. What we used in the past didn't create the life we want, so let's change it to something that will:

> ## "Success is created by achieving goals, where the results always feel like *great accomplishments*."

I've talked about great accomplishments since the Introduction, and success doesn't get any simpler. A great accomplishment is a personal achievement we design as the focus of our goal, and it drives us to reach the highest level of performance we can *at that time,* and *in that area of our lives*.

We normally think about setting goals for school, career, fitness, and making money, but great accomplishments work for anything we're trying to improve. They push us to exceed our levels of success from the past, which is how to transform our lives over and over. It's also how to feel a sense of power and control we've never had, because we'll know exactly what we're trying to accomplish at all times.

➢ If you're a student, how much greater could your GPA become?

➢ If you're a graduate starting a career, how much easier would it be to choose the right job in the right industry?

➢ And if you're in the middle or late stages of your working life, how would great accomplishments help you maximize your remaining years of income?

We need great accomplishments to maximize all areas of our lives, and when we do it benefits us in three ways:

1. Achieving them means reaching our best performances each time.

2. Feeling accomplished creates a motivation to achieve more and challenge ourselves at higher levels each time.

3. Those successes encourage us to work smarter, and faster, which means more efficiently.

Efficiency is vital because we all have limits on our time, money, and other resources. Being efficient means we'll succeed faster and more often in the same period of time, and living that way feels like a great accomplishment by itself. We also need to start thinking of success like a journey we're on, instead a destination we get to and stop.

Designing our lives to achieve great accomplishments is how to make our journey the best it can be, and that gives us a sense of purpose we can't get other ways. It also makes us feel like I talked about in Chapter 1, that we were **Born to Succeed.**

But How Do I Find Great Accomplishments? Whenever I talk to people about great accomplishments, they understand the concept pretty quickly. But as soon as they do, they want to know *how* to figure out what theirs are. We weren't trained to think that way as kids, and it's a skill that most of us never developed as adults.

To find your great accomplishments, all you need to do is think about the things that would reward you at the highest levels when you achieve them. Then you do that for each area of your life you want to improve. That might sound like dreaming, but it's actually designing. To succeed you have to give yourself permission to think this way, and as it becomes more comfortable your life starts to transform into what you want it to be.

At school, a great accomplishment might be getting into advanced classes, where in the gym it could be increasing your deadlift by 100 pounds. In your career, there might be a type of job that would fulfill you the most, or a promotion that will take you in a new and better direction.

Finding great accomplishments becomes simple once you focus on imagining exactly what you want, versus what you *think* you can accomplish.

Once you figure out your great accomplishments, it's much easier to design the goals needed to make those ideas your reality. Nothing great can happen by thinking safely, or doing the same things you've always done, so you have to spend time imagining the greatest things you can. Over time, as you change, your wants and needs will change too. The ability to imagine your great accomplishments is how to always be in pursuit of your greatest successes, and your greatest life.

Later we'll talk about how to design our goals to achieve greater things, but for now understand that simply thinking about what we want is the first skill we need to learn and practice. There might be some trial and error when we do, but that's how we improve. We need to practice until this feels like a natural extension of us, instead of something new and awkward.

And don't worry if you don't have clear answers right now, because we're going to talk about great accomplishments and designing our goals throughout the book. For now, instead of thinking about **how it might work,** let's start by simply imagining exactly **what we want** without any fear that "*It*" might not work.

No Substitue for Real Success: While we're deciding on our goals and great accomplishments, we have to be careful. Sometimes, in the pursuit of making changes and feeling accomplished, we can fall into a trap.

When we haven't had great accomplishments and success in the past it can feel like there's an empty space inside us, we need to fill. While we're improving ourselves, it's tempting to buy things that make us feel like we've accomplished something. We have to learn to see when that happens and recognize it as a *signal* that we're not focused on the right things.

When our great accomplishments are not the right ones, they don't automatically guide our actions like we need. At that point, it's easy to start filling that empty space with external rewards. Things like shopping for unneeded or expensive items are what I mean, and it's so common people jokingly call it *Retail Therapy*. But in my experience, it should be called *The Game of Substitution.*

It seems like instinct for us to use substitutes like clothes, cars, and vacations to make ourselves feel better, even if it's only temporary. But there's a danger when we do that, and when I said "*in my experience*" I meant the five times in nine years I bought a car to feel better about my lack of success. I was stuck in a loop of working for money to feel successful, but never getting there.

To fill in the empty space I didn't know was there, I bought cars to feel like I had control over something. I also didn't sell the one I already had, and carried two car loans because I could afford to. That not only cost me money I shouldn't have spent but took me further away from real accomplishments and success. But while I was doing it I got some satisfaction and self-esteem, which felt a lot like a great accomplishment.

Eventually I quit buying cars, but that wasn't the end of my substitutions. When I worked in IT sales, I bought a $3,000 Swiss watch to try and "*look more successful*" like my sales guys did. I was a Sales Engineer, and my job was designing computer networks for our customers, but I wanted to be seen as something more than just a fancy mechanic.

My customers never cared about my "*look*," but I still thought I needed to appear more accomplished. I learned the hard way that's not how success works, and that the "*fake it til you make it,*" or "*flex until you make it*" techniques are a lie. People have a good sense of who and what you are, so you will get found out and it won't end the way you want.

The best part of my story is that my "*fake it*" strategy was too weak to play the game the right way. I couldn't afford the $10,000 watches my sales guys had, so I ended up buying a *substitute,* for the *substitute,* for the success I wasn't creating with great accomplishments. I hoped the cheaper watch would be "*good-enough,*" and make me feel more accomplished, but I was dead wrong.

Looking back the idea was a waste of money, and the kind of thing I should be embarrassed to talk about it. But I'm not, because it's important to understand what we do, and how to see it before we spend our money. I'm not the only one who has done this, either, and my $3,000 mistake is identical to your $199 one, or someone else's million-dollar waste of money.

They're all equals in the Game of Substitution.

That's because they're all *signals* that tell us we're failing to create accomplishments. We're always looking for ways to fill that empty space inside us, though that's another thing we never learned as kids. Now is the time to see it, and stop ourselves using *Retail Therapy* as a tool for feeling successful. When we catch ourselves wanting to buy a substitution, it's time to review our goals to figure out what needs fixing, and how to get ourselves back on a successful path.

But I'm not saying you can't buy whatever you like, and pay whatever it costs, because that's none of my business. However, if you do that before you succeed enough financially, to justify what you're spending, you probably need to have a talk with yourself about substitutions.

In Chapter 8, we'll learn about the obstacles that keep us from starting or finishing our goals, because when that happens, we can get triggered to buy a substitute to fill the gap.

But How Great Is Great? I want to pause here a moment and clarify that great accomplishments don't have to be big or happen once in a lifetime to earn the title of Great. As long as they're your best performance at that time, in that area of your life, you're doing them correctly.

When you change your life to work that way, you'll find that success is always the ultimate outcome. I know that sounds like marketing again, but it's not. I don't mean you'll never experience a setback or failure, but you'll stop wanting to quit because your accomplishments will be so clear. Your path to achieve them will be well defined, and in my experience, we only give up on things we don't know the value of, or don't believe we could ever achieve.

That's why real failure can't happen until we decide to *stop trying*.

Goal Setting Redefined: Because great accomplishments create a clear vision for what our goals are meant to achieve, we need to think of goals in a different way. We've used the term "*goal setting*" our whole life, without understanding they're not just one simple thing. Most people think of the end result they want, and the actions needed to achieve it as one big concept. We call it "*our goal*" without knowing that we should define the **result** and the **action** parts separately.

That's because we don't always know the right actions to take and assume that we'll figure it out as we go. But when we can't, we start to lose motivation. It's also how we get results that aren't quite what we wanted or become overwhelmed by the process and feel we aren't good enough to finish. That's the worst, because once we decide we aren't the *type of person* who can complete that goal, we stop trying.

To fix that, we have to split our goals into two sections:

1. Accomplishments, and
2. Actions.

We have to start with a clear idea of what we're working for, to make sure it's going to be a great accomplishment when we achieve it. Then we work backwards, to identify the actions we need to get us there.

But we also need to know they're the *right* actions, because too often we do things we think should work, without really knowing. We also take advice from family and friends, who recommend strategies they heard second (or third) hand from other people. Using information we only think will work is not the way to create our successes with any precision.

Instead, I'm going to show you how to prove that the information you're using will work for your situation the first time. And when we separate the actions we take from the accomplishments we want, and prove they're the right ones for us, it changes the idea of setting a goal into *designing one*.

> ➤ Setting implies you know what you're doing, and just set the process in motion.

> ➤ Designing means investigating the process each time, to make sure you know what you're working for, what the right actions are to take, and the skills needed to achieve success.

You wouldn't build a house without a blueprint, so why would you work on a goal that you don't have a proven plan for? That's how we waste our time, money, and other resources, which is how we created the lives we're living in right now.

It's not that we can't do more for ourselves; it's that we don't understand how to plan for success by being clear on the accomplishments and the right actions.

Example of Goal Setting: "*I want to run a 5k someday.*"

That's a typical vague goal statement, and the kind we hear from people all the time. It doesn't tell us anything specific, and the details about the accomplishment section are missing. Nothing about that statement would call you into action, because you don't know how fast to run, where the race takes place, or when it will be held. And "*someday,*" like "*later,*" is also not found on any calendar, so before you even got started, you'd be doomed to fail.

Actually, you'd be doomed to sit on the couch because you didn't use any specifics to change your behavior and call you into action. That's why it's not actually a goal at all. Instead, it's just a vague statement of intent that's easy to give up on. That makes it more like a wish than a goal.

However, when we ***design*** a goal, it looks and feels much different.

Example of Goal Design: "*On Thanksgiving Day, 2020, I'm going to run the Turkey Trot 5k race in Fairfax. And I'll do it in under an hour.*"

That calls you to action and empowers you to plan for a specific result immediately. You know the details of the accomplishment section, which is 5 kilometers in under sixty minutes, in Fairfax, on Thanksgiving Day 2020. From there, you can easily figure out the Proven Actions needed to get you there, which in this case is simple:

Train for a pace of 19 minutes per mile or less, to finish in under an hour.

5k = 3.1 miles, divided into 59 minutes = 19 minute per mile pace.

If you find that's your best ability *at that time*, it qualifies as a great accomplishment, and where your training needs to start.

That's how we design our goals the right way the first time and avoid failures from not knowing what we're doing. It's also how to avoid unrealistic goals that demand a higher level of skill or preparation than we currently have. Don't get me wrong; we have to push past our limits to achieve our next levels of skill and accomplishment, however, we have to prove those things too, so we don't set ourselves up for avoidable frustrations and failures.

That's how simple it can be to design a goal for yourself that results in a great accomplishment. The process also works this way for more complicated goals, with some additional techniques that we'll discuss in Chapter 8. Once you start doing this, you'll see how easy it is, and how you can't fail until you stop trying.

Why? Because you'll always know what the standards are for succeeding. You're the one who defines them from the beginning, which means you're always the boss.

Changing Your Design: In the case of the Turkey Trot, if you train correctly, you'll meet or exceed the 19 minute per-mile time. If you find that you can't, you'll know to get help before race day. Changing training techniques is common for all athletes and knowing that during the design process of your goal keeps you from thinking you can't succeed and have to give up.

Along the way, if you decide that isn't what you want to do, you've discovered that running a 5k in less than an hour *isn't your great accomplishment*. That's the best part of this technique, because our goals shouldn't focus on anything else.

If you ever realize yours are not focused in the right places, or for the right reasons, you need to STOP. Again, you don't want to waste any of your limited time, money, or other resources that could be used for achieving goals that end in great accomplishments.

Sometimes, we design a goal that is totally valid today, but then change our minds later. That's perfectly fine, and it's better to find out sooner to avoid any feelings of failure that might keep you from designing goals at all. When you start living with that type of mental and emotional agility, you feel more accomplished and successful *immediately* from the control you get. The challenges you face won't matter as much, because you'll be empowered to design around, or through them, in a way you couldn't before.

The only reason we get overwhelmed is when it's hard to see all the pieces of the puzzle and get or goals organized in a way that we can drive them to successful outcomes. To remove that pressure, and make it easy from the start, we need to separate goals into ***accomplishment*** and ***action*** sections. That gives us the clarity we need so that the work we put in does the most for us the first time.

What's My Next Goal? Back to running for a moment. When you finish that Turkey Trot in less than an hour, your next level up might be doing a 5k race in 45 minutes. That means re-calculating your per-mile pace, and training to run at that speed. And if you find that 51 minutes is your best time, then that becomes your great accomplishment until you have more time to get faster or different techniques to do it sooner.

That's how simple this process is, and once you achieve a great accomplishment in any area of your life you need to think about designing the next one. In fact, while you're working on one today you should be thinking about what your next level up is, and how soon you need to design it. All our goals and skills development should be thought of that way, like a ***Continual Design Process*** that we prove to ourselves as we go. That's how to make sure we're creating the life we most want, without taking unproven actions that might not get us there.

Now imagine if we had this knowledge at the age of 10 and had been practicing this lifestyle since then. How much different would our personal, professional, and financial successes be right now? We can't travel back in time to change anything, but we can start to make changes to create our futures on purpose. And since thinking and designing are free, we don't have anything holding us back.

Designing Your Career: Before we leave the topic of goal design, I want to talk about how we build our careers. We already know that our first few jobs—often chosen randomly—tend to dictate the types of jobs and industries we stay in. As a result, our personal, professional, and financial successes can be limited without us realizing why. Staying in the same jobs and industries has been the norm for the last 70 years, but that doesn't mean we should keep doing it.

Remember the Gallop poll? Fewer than one person in four is satisfied in his/her current job. That should be all the proof you need that remaining in a career or industry where you're not happy isn't a reasonable or productive choice.

Most companies don't guide their employees through any meaningful career development, so we're on our own to design that. We need a clear plan for exactly what we want, and the mental agility to make changes when necessary. Otherwise, it's easy to find ourselves in places we don't love, without a plan or the confidence for how to leave.

The good news is that goal design is the same whether we work for ourselves, for others, or we're hustling to do both. The most important thing is deciding on the right skills to develop, and the jobs and industries we should work in. That way, the size and speed of our successes don't get limited by anyone but us.

And I know how exactly how that feels, because the first 15 years of my career were limited by poor choice-making. I developed skills that kept paying me more, but I wasn't progressing as an IT professional and had no clue that I should be. I didn't know what building a career meant, so I kept working in task-worker jobs, expecting someone or something to elevate me to a better position "*later.*"

The worst part is it turned me into the kind of employee that bosses can count on but will never promote. I didn't look like a guy who was promotable, so I was never offered the chance to move up. And I was so ignorant to how the process worked that nothing seemed to be wrong. They kept paying me well as my engineering skills improved, and I kept equating my paycheck with success.

The reality is I gave away my best years of career building to the wrong skills, the wrong jobs, and the wrong industries. Money was my only guiding force, and what it really did was hold me back from discovering my great accomplishments and achieving them.

Those were the years I felt so empty, and why I bought so many cars to fill that space. Looking back, I have to wonder how much personal and financial success I missed out on by not knowing better. Frankly, it's painful to think about. That's why driving our careers with a purpose is so important, and why we need a continual goal-design process to do it. It's the only way to achieve the income we want today, and the retirement we want for the future.

So, ask yourself this:

<h2 style="text-align:center">If I don't design my career
and my future, who will?</h2>

To help you get started creating or retooling your career, I created a checklist:

1. Identify your great accomplishments, the skills you love using, and the jobs and industries that pay you the most to use them.

2. Continue improving those skills to maximize your accomplishments and income.

3. Use a continual design process to review your accomplishments, and make sure they're always driving you to achieve what you want.

4. Be ready to change your skills, jobs, and industries when change is needed.

5. Be humble, be a learner, and *be honest with yourself.*

Number five will be the hardest for some, because things like fear, uncertainty, and doubt get in the way of being honest and making changes. Learning about pillar number three is going to fix that for us, so don't worry because we're going to get there.

Everyone's goal is to have the kind of life they most want to live, and it really is this simple when you follow the checklist, and continually eliminate unsuccessful things from your life.

Section 3 - Accomplishments, Goals, and Actions Must Be Proven.

Olympic athletes are a great example of how proving our great accomplishments, goal designs, and actions will drive our successes beyond what we've done in the past.

Not only are Olympians the most accomplished in their sport, but they train for four years between the Olympic games to stay that way. And unlike professional athletes, they don't have as many games to compete in to keep their competitive edge. That means their mental strategy for training is much different, to keep them focused for that many years.

Dedication like that shows how **Great Accomplishments**, **Proven Actions** that work for us, and a **Goal Design** are the right **Recipe for Success**.

The Best Swimmer You Can Be: Imagine you were a great swimmer as a teen and wanted to push your skills and performance to qualify for the Olympics. Would it make any sense to add running workouts to your training schedule? It might, and running is good for building strength and stamina, but how would you know if it was right for you?

You would need facts that *prove* it gets you to your swimming accomplishments faster, and/or at higher levels of performance. If you didn't know that before you began, you would be wasting your limited training time on actions with an unproven "*payment.*"

Even if running was a good technique for swimmers in general, you would still have some questions to answer:

> ➤ What kind of running is best for me?

> ➤ How do I prove that?

Running is a diverse activity, and there are sprints, stairs, intervals, hills, or a combination of them that people use for different results. Until you knew the *best choice for you*, you would only get a partial payment for your efforts because you would be guessing about the right choices. To protect ourselves from doing random stuff, we need to do research to prove that the information we think is right for us actually is.

And proving things needs to be our mindset all day long, to make sure our thoughts and actions get us closer to our great accomplishments. Since the Internet is one of the best tools for doing research, we have to understand how the process really works.

Just Google It: How many times have we heard this, or said it ourselves? But if I asked you to explain how a Google search works behind the scenes, could you do it?

Most people can't, and it's not a fair question to ask, but understanding how to use the results is something we can all learn. When we use any search engine, the answers on the first page are divided into three categories:

1. Paid advertisements at the top of the list, with the word "**Ad**" next to them.

2. Paid placements which come next, but don't have the word Ad next to them.

3. The most selected items from recent searches on the topic you're looking for.

The advertisements we can ignore, because they're only trying to sell us something. That leaves the paid placements and most recent searches, which you might think are the best for our needs. But that's not always true, and it's dangerous to think that way.

Those answers are there because they've been "*optimized*" to show up at the top of the list, or they've been driven there by people clicking on them in the past. An answer's position at (or near) the top of the list doesn't mean that it's accurate, only popular. That's why we can't use them without seeing if they're from a source we can trust. If we don't know who those sources are yet, that becomes our first proving task.

In our swimming and running example, a credible source for training advice might be online magazines for swimmers and runners. They have articles on training techniques every year, but I would still verify those with sources like university or medical journal studies on that kind of training. It's not hard to get value from scientific papers, even if you're not a scientist. And because there's so much bad information and opinion on the Internet, you have to know how to protect yourself from it.

Knowing what's real—versus what's popular—is a critical skill we need for our proving process, and like every new skill, we must practice to become better at it.

The Rule of Threes: When I do research, I use a technique called The Rule of Threes that I learned from a former U.S. Navy SEAL. When they plan missions, they try to verify the information they're working with from three independent sources. That's how they prove if it's real, has the value they think it does, and most importantly *where it stops helping them*. To increase their levels of safety and success, to the highest they can be *at that time*, they've got to do the research.

And that's no different than what we're doing. The information we use will only be helpful until we or something in our life changes, so we need to be clear about when that value goes away. That's why I keep saying "*at that time,*" because transforming our lives means being able to deal with change when the information we're working with changes. Having three credible sources makes our goal designs as strong they can be at that time, until something tells us to redesign them.

Thankfully, we'll need to redesign less often as our skills improve, so it's not like we'll be making changes every day. And the greatest feeling is when changes aren't necessary because our designs are created so well. To me, that feeling is almost as rewarding as the great accomplishment our goal is designed for in the first place.

Again, success is a journey we're on, and techniques like goal design make it a reward in itself.

When SEALs go on a mission, design and change management is their focus. Because changes happen unexpectedly, they have to be ready to redesign plans and actions quickly. Sometimes that means cancelling the mission, but more than likely it means using a Plan B they prepared before they got started. Because they often get only one chance to be successful, they have to deal with whatever circumstances they find when they get where they're going.

President Teddy Roosevelt has a famous quote that sums this up:

> *"Do what you can, with what you have, where you are."*

We need to think in the same way, which the SEALs call being "*Mission Focused.*" Since our goals are designed to achieve an accomplishment that will be great for us, we could say that's our Mission, and the only thing we should focus on. That's how to achieve increasing levels of success, by never quitting, and always finding the answers we need.

Once we design a goal there shouldn't be a question about what we want, or if we can get there, just how to get it done and when we can. A former SEAL officer I met explained how a Plan B lifestyle is normal for them, and he gave me an example of that with this question:

"How long does it take to plan a SEAL mission?"

I had no idea, and what he told me was big surprise: "*10 minutes more than you have.*"

That's a joke in the SEAL community, because in the high-speed world of Special Operations warfare that's the reality they're often faced with. There is never enough information on their side when they want it, so they have to do the best they can with what they have and keep researching as the mission progresses.

Improving their rate of success and survival is about being better and faster with thinking, designing, and changing skills. Thankfully, we don't have the same pressure to perform, but we can take a lesson from them, and the way they plan and act. By practicing our thinking, designing, and changing skills every day we'll have bigger and faster victories too. We'll save time and frustration by researching and proving the information we need, before we get started. That's how to take the right actions the first time and correct any problems in the fastest way.

By being mission focused we won't need to stop when something changes, we'll just regroup and redesign our plan to get back on our mission. And since no one will be shooting at us, we'll have a much easier time than the SEALs do.

Qualifying Your Resources: When we do research, which includes the information we get from other people, we have to ask questions about the value it brings us. In other words, what type of "*Resource*" are we working with? A resource is anything that brings us value, like a tool, information, or a person who helps us with their time, knowledge, and skills.

I said before we can't take advice from people until we prove whether it will work for our needs, but what about the guidance we receive from experts and mentors? Will they always be helpful to us, and if so, how do we prove *that*?

We have to look at **all** the information we deal with to see if it's a resource for us, and then qualify it further to make sure we know how and when to use it in our goal designs.

And it only takes three Qualifying Questions:

1. Does this information/person/tool help me?
2. In what way does it help me?
3. For how long will it help me?

Question one is a simple Yes or No, where we decide if someone or something can help us. An example from my life was when I decided to quit my job to start my own business.

Nobody I knew had experience doing that, so the advice they gave me wasn't a resource. They didn't know how to help me as an Entrepreneur, or guide me in my goal designs, so from the perspective of creating greater success in my life I couldn't use their advice.

I know they wanted the best for me, but they simply didn't have the skills and experience I needed. It's normal to encourage and support the people we care about, but the lesson here is that not every source of support is actually useful as a resource.

Sometimes the people we know will insert themselves into our journey without asking and try to guide us with their opinions and experience. You have to be clear with yourself, and with them, as to whether they can help you or not. Just like an article on the Internet that you prove the value of, you have to prove the value of the people who want to help you.

Question two is where we figure out the way in which a resource can help us. In our Olympic swimming example, running would help us become a better swimmer if we could prove it with books, articles, or coaches that we trust. And there are many running techniques to improve our strength, distance, and stamina. After proving that the source of the information was valid for our needs, we would then prove the technique(s) that would help us the most in the pool.

If the value we gain from a resource is not as big as we need, then we have to look for a better one. It's true you can dig a swimming pool with a shovel, but it's not the best resource to get the job done.

Question three is usually the easiest to answer, because once we identify a resource, and the way it can help us, the last question is *"for how long."*

Running shoes are a great example, because they're rated by how many miles they're good for like car tires. The average rating for running shoes is 400 miles, which for some of us would mean a lifetime of use. However, a runner who trains for 100-kilometer races, which is 62 miles, may need multiple pairs every year. For their goal designs, the *"for how long"* part of the same resource is much different than most.

The need to classify our resources might sound weird, especially as it pertains to the people we know, but it's a game-changer, and something we must do. It helps us make the best decisions we can in our continual design process, and because things can change unexpectedly, we have to keep these questions in mind all the time. Knowing we need to change direction is important and having this talk with ourselves is more of the practice we need to become an expert at designing our goals.

Time for A Break: While we're transforming ourselves, and researching and proving everything, we also need to think about time off. We can't focus on goals all the time, even though I said earlier we need to. What I meant was that we need to focus on all the right things we should be doing, while eliminating the wrong ones.

However, being overly focused can create frustration and mistakes, and become a different problem for us. So, I'm not asking you go at this fast, but I am asking you to go. You don't have to change your actions immediately, but you can change your *mindset* right now. That can be changed today, to start guiding your discovery of great accomplishments, finding the proof you need for the actions to take, and qualifying your resources to maximize your results.

What I'm sharing here is that when you have a clear vision for being your most accomplished, you get an immediate feeling of control in your life. You also get control of your happiness and success, because you start limiting your exposure to the things that don't help you get those.

And there's an added bonus to all this. That process of becoming clearer and more efficient is how to find new levels of accomplishment much faster. Then, when you take time off, it won't feel like you're wasting any time or losing out on achieving successes. When you need a break, you'll know where you stopped in your process, how to restart, and what to expect when you do.

That's how to feel Mission Focused.

It's like pausing a movie and returning later to continue watching. With movies we don't have to start over, or give up watching, because we still know the *who, what, when, where,* and *why* parts of the story. Since you're now the creator of *your story*, you'll know what you're doing, what comes next, and how to **prove** it all to be sure.

And if any of this sounds overwhelming, take a pause. If you're not sure you can do all of this I understand, because I was in the same place as you since I was 15 years old. No one taught me about goals, great accomplishments, or creating the life I wanted, so I drifted along without a purpose and felt lost.

Eventually I developed a career that lasted nearly 22 years, but it always felt like the world was this unchangeable collection of standards I had to meet without knowing how to. I didn't realize that I could create my own world and have this kind of control until I was in my forties.

But I did it, and you can too.

In the next chapter we'll talk about transforming further with our second Pillar of Success, called *Personal Identity*. Once we have great accomplishments to guide us, and the right goal designs to achieve them, becoming the *type of person* who can take those actions is the next step.

So, don't feel any pressure to perform right now. Focus on changing your mindset and opening up to the idea that this is possible. Thinking about great accomplishments and designing your goals is free, and you can practice those skills until you're ready to take action.

This will work for you once you start proving things to yourself, and while you're doing that keep this quote in mind:

A thousand-mile journey begins with the first step.

Get Ready to Take Yours.

CHAPTER 4

Pillar Two - Personal Identity

Personal Identity, P.I. for short, is the term Psychologists use when talking about different types of people. They define it this way:

> *"The traits and characteristics, social relations, roles, and social group memberships that define us, are the components of Personal Identity."*

We all have a P.I., and ours tells us not only **Who we think we are**, but more importantly **What we think we can do**. That means our accomplishments are both created by, and limited from, our P.I.

To transform our life into the one we most want, we first have to learn **how** to change.

We're going to look at Personal Identity in three ways, to understand what it is, what it does, and how it's such a powerful tool for creating success:

1. How P.I. was created.

2. P.I.'s have Boundaries and Speed Limits.

3. How to change our P.I. to achieve greater success.

Section 1 - How P.I. Was Created

As children we learned about the *traits* and *characteristics* mentioned in the definition, and we did it by watching how our families, friends, and everyone around us interacted. Our instincts told us that was very important, and by the time we went to Kindergarten we understood why.

Traits and characteristics taught us to predict how people would behave. Over time, we saw that some behaviors were always grouped together into "*types of people*," and how they did the same things in predictable ways. Everyone referred to those types using *labels*, and that's how we learned to do it.

He's Nice. She's mean. He's scary. She's funny.

Those are some of the basics we started with as kids, and as we got older, our labels for people became more detailed. Labels helped us understand who our friends and foes were, and by middle school, we and our classmates had labeled everyone we knew. That's how we determined which *type of person* we were becoming, and the social groups we could fit into. *Jocks, Nerds, Preppies,* and *Band Geeks* are a few of the P.I. labels I grew up with, and every generation has their own.

Throughout high school and college, the labels we accepted from others, and the ones we gave ourselves, formed, reformed, and determined what our final P.I. would be. And unless someone or something taught us that we could change our identity in a specific way, we didn't.

As an adult, you might think the days of labeling are over, and we've grown beyond them, but we haven't. If you look at how you think of (and talk about) other people, labeling has only gotten worse.

We still use them to define and understand other people, and ourselves, and for two very good reasons.

1. We need a quick method to understand *types of people.*
2. Labeling is the universal method.

Soccer moms, Millennials, Newlyweds, and Veterans.

Familiar terms like those immediately remind us of the traits and behaviors that we associate with those types of people. That's how powerful P.I. labels are, and why they're a great shortcut to help us deal with the people we meet. And if one label doesn't paint the whole picture, we can use as many as we need until they do.

> He's a *"Retired" "Army Guy"* with a *"PhD"* in math. But really, he's more like a *"Sales Guy"* turned *"Investor"* who works in biotech. And he's *"Gay."*

It took six P.I. labels to describe that man, and really eight if you count math and biotech. At that point, you might feel like you know enough about him to predict his behavior, but you also might be wrong.

The picture in your head is based on your *opinion* of those labels, which may not be accurate in the end. Until you get to know him, you're using limited information to make a judgment. But that's how our decision-making process works. In the blink of an eye we use what we know in that moment, based on what we knew in the past.

That's why we sometimes like people more when we forget about the labels and get to know them.

The P.I. Problem: We also judge ourselves using the same technique that we use to judge other people, but it's not any more accurate. In the blink of an eye, we decide the goals we can design, the actions we can take, and the accomplishments we believe *"a person like us"* can achieve.

That's how powerful Personal Identity is, and why it's the second *Pillar of Success.* All of our decisions are made from that perspective, which is another reason why our lives are where they are right now.

I Can't Go to The Race: In 2011, a friend invited me to participate in one of those obstacle course races in the mud. I had never done one before, or any kind of race for that matter, and it struck me as a ridiculous idea. In fact, I was sure an event like that would kill me, because at the time I weighed about 285 pounds.

At six feet tall that was 85 pounds more than I should have been, and my P.I. stepped in to save me by saying:

"Fat Guys can't do that."

Fat Guys can't run races, climb over 8-foot walls, and get through five kilometers of muddy challenges in the 90-degree heat of July. Everyone knows that, so why would you invite a Fat Guy to a race?

That's how our P.I. protects us from danger, but also keeps us from achieving greater success. Once we think we know *who we are,* we think we know *what we can do,* and we don't go any further. Our P.I. keeps us from proving anything to ourselves, and instead says we're fine where we are.

Think about that in comparison to the P.I. you think you have today: Teen Athlete, New College Graduate, or Middle Manager. Whomever you identify as defines the actions you feel able to take, and those feelings won't change while you think *your identity is true,* and *your identity is you.*

As a Fat Guy I *"knew"* it was ridiculous for me to run in a race, so I called my friend to tell him I couldn't *"see myself doing that."* And that's a common thing to think and feel, because our P.I. tells us when we aren't the *type of person* who can do things we see as risky.

But my friend wouldn't take no for an answer. He insisted that I could complete the race with help, how four of us would work as a team, and that no one would be left behind. He also said it wasn't a race you had to run, and people walked as much of it as they needed to.

Since I was free to quit if the challenge was too much, I agreed to go.

Completing it took more than two hours, but to my surprise became one of the greatest accomplishments of my life. And I was so excited when I saw the finish line that I actually sprinted the last 50 feet to cross it. Wearing my medal at the finish line made me feel like an Athlete, because I overcame physical and mental challenges I never knew I could.

For the prior 15 years I had been depressed about my lack of accomplishments without knowing it and expected nothing could change. I comforted myself with food as a substitute, which meant I had to adopt the Fat Guy P.I. to protect myself and make it all seem normal.

But standing there, covered in mud, I realized my *"Fat Guy"* time was over. For the first time in my life, at the age of 43, I saw that having a goal and achieving it was always **a matter of choice**. It felt like a giant emotional weight was lifted off me, and I could think and move freely again.

And in that moment, I couldn't remember why I had turned my friend down, and why I'd been so afraid to go.

Years later, the answer became clear. To protect ourselves from embarrassment and failure, our internal *"safety mechanism"* keeps us from taking risks beyond what our P.I. thinks we can handle. It also gives us a bunch of excuses to hide behind, that others are used to hearing.

"I'm too old; not athletic; not that type of person."

The list is endless, and when I got invited to the race, I thought it was obvious *who I was*, and what my answer would be:

"I'm just a Fat Guy, and we can't do that."

When things seem risky, we often think they can only lead to failure because of who we think we are. That label we use to describe ourselves determines what we think we can do, and then our safety mechanism takes over to stop us from changing. We don't have a built-in *"proof mechanism"* to help us discover how much more we can accomplish, so we often don't try. Picking things that seem safer is the default choice for most of us, and it feels totally normal every time we do it.

There's also a sound that the safety mechanism makes, and I'll bet you've heard it:

"Better safe than sorry."

Not only do people say that to us, but we've learned to say it to ourselves and to others. It's so simple, and it sounds so obvious, that we think of it as *"**common sense**."* But it's another *Illusory Truth* that we all adopted without any proof of its accuracy or its usefulness.

Knowing what I know now, our commonly accepted safety mechanism sounds more like this to me:

"You don't know what you're doing, and you shouldn't try."

What *"better safe than sorry"* really means is that we should only choose things we know to be safe, and let others take risks. But if that were the best way to live our lives, how did we overcome the risk of great bodily harm and death to learn to drive a car?

First, it's something everyone does, so everyone sees it as normal. After that we eliminated any feelings of risk the same way we do for any great accomplishment: Exposure, Skills, and Passion.

➤ **Exposure** - We rode in cars our whole life, which told us it was normal to drive. Every adult did it, and we were told by them that we could too.

➤ **Skills** - We took a driver's education class and had time to practice with the family car. That's how we improved our skills to the levels we needed to be safe behind the wheel.

➤ **Passion** - We wanted our license more than anything else at the time, and we were willing to do whatever it took to get there. We didn't know it back then, but driving was an early great accomplishment for us.

If you look at any skill you've developed, and any obstacles you've overcome, your path to success was always created that way: Exposure, Skills, and Passion.

The more we know about things, **called proof**, the less risky they feel. Then with the right skills and practice our passion always drives us to succeed. That's the technique to improve everything in our lives and having great accomplishments as our mission focus creates the passion we've been missing.

I didn't cross the finish line in 2011 because I was an athlete that day. I crossed because I refused to quit. The reward I got drove me to compete in more challenging races over the years, which I prepared for by becoming the *type of person* I needed to each time. Since 2011, I've done seven obstacle course races and the Marine Corps 10k race three times. That's how I know this process works, and how making a change in our lives is that simple.

You can do this too, and you don't have to go fast when you do it.

But you do have to go.

To create a new life, with the skills you need for continued success, you have to get started. The good news is that thinking about and designing your changes is all that getting started means. We think that making changes means taking action to get results as quickly as possible, but it doesn't.

Rushing the process doesn't make it work any better, and without having the right goal design and the proof to support it, you won't know the right actions to take anyway. All you need today is the knowledge that P.I. exists, you can change it to become the person you need to be, and that we're going to get there in section 3 of this chapter.

Before we do, let's expand on how P.I. works, both for us and against, so that when we make changes, we won't get stuck at a level of accomplishment we only *think* is our best.

Section 2 - P.I.'s Have Boundaries and Speed Limits.

So far, we've covered five things about Personal Identity:

1. Behavioral *traits* are grouped together, into *types of people*.

2. Types are identified by P.I. *labels*, which are shortcuts we use to quickly understand each other.

3. Some labels are given to us, while others *we create ourselves*.

4. Our P.I. tells us, and others we know, *who we are*, and *what we're able to do*.

5. We can change our P.I. by deciding on *who we need to become*.

Next we have to talk about P.I. boundaries. Those are the limiters that affect our identities by telling us how much we can succeed as a certain type of person. Learning to change our P.I. doesn't mean we *unlearn* all the old behaviors we've had, so we need to understand what these boundaries are to see them before they limit our progress.

We Deserve A Break: When we complete a goal to earn a great accomplishment, it feels like we deserve a break for all our hard work. And we might, but there's a danger that we won't get restarted on our journey to success. I call that condition **Being on Pause Without A Plan**, which is easy to do when you've achieved something that feels so good. Pausing is normal, and people will say we've earned the right to do it. But being there without a schedule and a plan to get restarted is a BIG problem.

It creates a P.I. boundary we don't realize we're hitting, because it feels so normal to sit back and enjoy our accomplishments. However, success can be dependent on when we take action, so we have to think ahead to see what other successes we might be affecting by pausing.

Missing opportunities like that feels terrible, but they can be avoided by understanding that we have boundaries and how they affect us. It's easy to forget how long we've been on pause without a date to get back to work, and a new great accomplishment to work for. But that's not how success is created, so thinking about and designing your next two or three accomplishments is where your thoughts need to be.

That way, while you're pausing, you'll know exactly what else you've got to do. By making a schedule you'll also know when to come back, based on the needs of the accomplishments you just decided on.

Our Safety Mechanism Never Stops: Part of transforming our lives means clearly defining the P.I. for the *type of person* we want to become, like *Runner*. But in that moment our safety mechanism will try to keep us from "*going too far,*" or "*doing too much,*" which means we could change our opinion of what that P.I. really means. And until we get more practice, it could feel like any other decision we make and go unnoticed.

That's another P.I. boundary that says what we've created is "*good enough,*" or we can just "*try this new thing out*" to see what might happen. But there's no such thing as "*trying out*" success, there are only great accomplishments, proven actions, and your mission focus to do the work.

Unfortunately, when our safety mechanism takes over the P.I. creation process we can feel the urge to scale down our efforts. We can use smaller or easier "*versions*" of that P.I. without realizing it. Since P.I.'s are defined by the skills we develop, we have to fight back so that we don't retreat toward safety. Otherwise, we end up diluting the idea of who we need to become. To create our greatest accomplishments, our skills need to be at the highest levels we can create them at that time.

Anything less is failing ourselves before we begin, which is the **opposite** of why we're changing in the first place. But when our safety mechanism creates a boundary to think about less and do less, that's all we're going to get. And again, it happens so quietly we have to be looking for that urge to do less and stop it.

Right now, most of us have no way of knowing how "*far*" our skills or accomplishments can go. We haven't known how to test our limits in the past, and until we know how to prove everything how could we? I tell the people I mentor that until we fail consistently with improving ourselves, we haven't proven where "*far*" is. Until we reach that proven point of failure, we must keep going.

Once we find a point of failure we might need a coach or mentor who has gotten to where we want to be to help us push further. But if we don't know to ask, our safety mechanism will tell us it's all normal and we can stop. Since we don't know how far we can go it says this:

➢ Wait to see what happens.

➢ We can always change later.

➢ Someday we'll do this.

I ask myself this instead: "*When did waiting for later make me more successful?*"

The only acceptable answer is when we know exactly what we're doing, why we're waiting, and when to restart.

> ***"It is not the strongest species that survive, nor the most intelligent,
> but the ones most responsive to change." ~ Charles Darwin***

Becoming A Changemaker: When we create or upgrade our P.I., we need to understand it won't be the last time. We need to do a P.I. review periodically, and every time we create or change an accomplishment in our goal designs. That's the quickest way to know if that P.I. can support us, or if we need to change or upgrade our skills.

To become faster and better at making changes, we need to know how our knowledge is organized into three categories:

- **Category 1** - Things we know well and use all the time.

- **Category 2** - Things we don't know well and need to learn more about.

- **Category 3** - Things we have no awareness of.

Category 1 knowledge is what we've been talking about so far. We use it all the time, and it's the stuff that feels like our normal decision-making process. And now we know more about what it really is, and how it needs to be changed, so it should be easier to get started.

Category 2 knowledge is the kind we put off learning until we absolutely have to, which can go on for decades. Planning for retirement is a great example, because people know they need to learn more about it, but few know the right way to do it. Many people think contributing to a 401k plan is all you do, without ever proving how the process works.

The common mistake I learned, *by making it for 15 years,* is that you need a goal for the amount of money you want when you retire. Then you divide that by the number of years you have left to work, which tells you how much per year to invest. I think many people would agree they need to know more about their retirement plan, but never seem to get around to it.

Category 3 knowledge is the kind we've never heard of, and because of that is the biggest threat to our success. An example from my life was when my homeowner's association needed to make emergency repairs in our community and had no money set aside for it. The only choice was to charge each owner a *Special Assessment Fee* of $3,500. Thankfully they were able to let us pay on a monthly basis, but the concept was a shock to me in two ways.

1. I had no idea special assessments existed.

2. I wasn't prepared to pay triple my monthly association fees for the next year.

But I had no choice, even if I sold the house and moved. I was legally responsible for that cost, even though I didn't create the problem, or have any control over how it happened. That's the truth about living in a community with an owner's association, and why some say they would never do it again.

Categories 2 and 3 have so much power over us because we're often unprepared for them or know what they mean. But when those things change and affect us, we have to be ready to deal with them. That means avoiding denial and finding the way to get back to our mission. We can only ignore them for so long, and that timeframe becomes very short when we're dedicated to creating success.

On the positive side, our acceptance of a changing world opens us up to new possibilities, and new successes in the future. We don't want to miss opportunities and create regret for ourselves when it's so easy to avoid.

I worked in the Information Technology field for nearly 22 years before realizing it was no longer what I wanted. Looking back, it feels like I should have never been there, but when I started in 1996 my P.I. was very weak. Without knowing I could define my own accomplishments I borrowed some from friends in the industry and got started making money. That gave me a higher level of financial safety than I ever had, which to my untrained mind felt like success.

By 2018 I no longer "*saw myself*" having a future there, so I quit my job, and walked away from a big six-figure income. People thought I was crazy, but the money had stopped bringing value to me, and I needed something more. I was craving different accomplishments, so I shifted my focus to developing *The Framework Life* and dedicated myself to helping people transform themselves.

But two years earlier I was just "*another guy*" writing "*another book.*" I didn't have the vision for what this project would become, how it would evolve, or how it would change me. I had a bunch of category 2 and 3 knowledge to overcome, but my Changemaker skills were strong enough to carry me to success. They empowered me to deal with all the challenges I faced, without any P.I. boundaries getting in the way or stopping me.

Practicing Changemaker skills is how to keep boundaries from developing, and to keep from putting ourselves on pause without a plan. And you've already become a Changemaker if you know how to drive a car, because when you're driving there are also three categories of knowledge to deal with.

- **Category 1** - Road conditions.

- **Category 2** - Weather conditions.

- **Category 3 -** People conditions, which are the skills, levels of awareness, and behaviors of the drivers around us.

When we're driving, we have to pay attention to all three, and be ready if they change without warning. Something as simple as a slow rainfall becoming a downpour changes everything we do in an instant:

- ➤ We increase the speed on our windshield wipers.

- ➤ We slow down, to create distance between us and the car we're following.

- ➤ We pay closer attention to what the cars around us are doing.

Now you can see that if you're an accomplished driver, you're already an accomplished Changemaker too. That means you're able to create and manage changes in every area of your life, using the three pillars.

Companies like Uber, Netflix, and Tesla had to be experts in changemaking to become the leaders in their industries. That meant changing before their competitors did, or in the case of Uber, defining a new industry that no one knew they needed.

Before they existed, nobody would agree to get into a car with a stranger who wasn't a licensed taxi or limousine. Now it's the default mode of ground transportation for people in many countries, and even the word Uber has become a verb. The founders of Uber achieved that level of success by changing their Personal Identities to support those accomplishments and breaking through any boundaries that got in their way.

Personal Identity must evolve as our interests and lives require it, so that who we are and what we can do won't ever be an obstacle between us and greater success.

Speed Limits - Don't Let Anything Slow You Down.

Speed limits are part of our P.I. as well and come from believing we can only change ourselves or create successes at one speed. Even when our P.I. is strong, and we don't have boundaries telling us what we can do, we can get limited by thinking we need more time between accomplishments. And sometimes we think we can only change one area at a time, like school goals before work goals, and personal ones "*someday*" after that.

But again, where's the proof? The speed at which we can make changes, upgrade our skills, and achieve new accomplishments ***hasn't been determined yet***, so why are we putting speed limits on our success?

➢ How do we know how fast we can do things?

➢ How do we know how much can we do this week, month, or year?

➢ Most importantly, where did this fear come from that says to slow down?

My technique for eliminating speed limits is to *try and be wrong as fast as possible*. That might sound contradictory, but it's actually just thinking and designing. The faster I can prove what the wrong choices are for my goals, the easier it is to find the right ones. I'm always checking myself to see if there's a better, smarter, or easier way to achieve my accomplishments, so I can move myself forward as fast as possible. And just like paying attention while driving, checking your thoughts and actions all day becomes an extension of you when you practice.

To make sure I'm performing at my best, and avoiding boundaries and speed limits, I ask myself "*how do I know?*" That's the quickest way to prove things to yourself with one simple question, and until you have the right answer you have to keep looking for it. Otherwise it's easy to fall back on our feelings of safety. When we don't have proven accomplishments and actions, our fears will fill in the blanks by telling us how to run from success back into the arms of safety.

Better safe than sorry, you know.

No One Can Run That Fast: People have been measuring the per-mile pace of competitive runners since 1850. And for 104 years it was "*known*" that a human couldn't run a mile in under four minutes. That was the speed limit for the P.I. called "*Runner*," and was the accepted "*fact*" around the world. Everyone "*knew*" it was true, and there was no reason to doubt it.

But in 1954, Roger Bannister decided it was no longer *his fact* or *his speed limit* and ran a mile in 3 minutes and 59.4 seconds. Though it was only six tenths of a second faster than the "*known fact*," it was faster, and it did break the world record. It was also a new beginning that disproved a P.I. speed limit that *everyone* called Runner had agreed on. And since then, 13 other runners have broken the record by *going even faster*. As of 1999, the fastest time was reduced to 3 minutes and 43.13 seconds, which translates to a speed of more than 16 miles per hour.

For perspective, some dogs can run at 15 to 20 miles per hour in short bursts, so you can imagine how hard it is for a human to do it for nearly four minutes. But 14 runners have done it by ignoring the mental speed limit of the Runner P.I., and the 104-year belief that said it couldn't be done. Evidence like that shows us what we *think* and *know* about ourselves is not usually true, which is why I keep saying we have to find the proof.

Proof Is Key: We're all affected by boundaries and speed limits, so we have to practice seeing when they happen. Then we have to prove how much further we can go by creating new great accomplishments to work for.

Otherwise, when we have a success, we think we have the right to pause. And we might, if the following things are true:

➤ The achievement of our goal was a clearly-defined great accomplishment.

➤ We know our next levels of accomplishment to plan for.

➤ We know the timeframe to get started again.

Otherwise we stay on pause for too long and settle on that level of accomplishment for years. That's how our lives got to be the way they are right now, because we've been limited by boundaries and speed limits we didn't know about.

But now we do, and how easy they are to change once we decide they no longer represent *who we want to be*.

Section 3 - How To Change Our P.I. To Achieve Greater Success.

I said in Chapter 1 we were all born to succeed, and I truly believe that. We were supposed to have more successful lives than we do right now, but we didn't get the training and skills we needed to create them. So, like everyone around us, we did the best we could with the knowledge we had.

A famous quote from former Secretary of Defense Donald Rumsfeld sums this up:

"You go to war with the army you have,

not the army you might wish to have later."

That tells us we have to start our journey with the knowledge, skills, and resources we have today, and maximize the results we can with them. But we can't afford to stay there, because our knowledge, skills, and resources can only take us so far. We'll always need new P.I.'s to support our next great accomplishments, and the way to keep reinventing ourselves works like this:

1. Define detailed great accomplishments that push us to a higher level than before.

2. Identify the type of person who can earn those accomplishments, the skills we need to become that type, and the levels those skills need to be at.

3. Make a plan to create or improve those skills and start becoming that type of person.

4. Look for signals that say we've come to a boundary or speed limit.

5. Be a Changemaker, to keep adapting when change is needed.

6. Go back to step 1.

Living that way will keep you improving your life, by always becoming the next better version of yourself. But to be fair, I know it might sound oversimplified and I don't want this to feel like the Nike "***Just Do It!***" campaign.

I can't just say "*become the person you need to be*," or "*go get those skills*" without some context. So, here's my story for how I changed my P.I. from the *Fat Guy* to an *Athlete*.

After my 5k race in 2011, I decided that becoming an Athlete was what I wanted. To get there, I was going to join a Crossfit gym, and push myself to new levels of fitness. But like a lot of people, I thought I needed to lose weight first, and rebuild my strength, before going to the gym. I "*thought*" I wasn't ready for such intense workouts, and I didn't want to waste my time and money by failing and being embarrassed that I couldn't keep up.

Later I found that was totally wrong, because Crossfit is designed to adapt each exercise to a person's physical ability. But since I didn't do the research we talked about; I was failing from the start. I was afraid to go to a gym because I knew I couldn't perform like the "*real athletes*."

This is a perfect example of failing with Category 2 information you don't know *enough* about and putting yourself on pause without a plan to get restarted. I told myself I would "*figure it out later*" when I lost "*some weight*."

But as I've said, no one knows when "*later*" comes, and no one can tell me how much "*some weight*" is either. Unfortunately, that's how we think and talk when we don't have a two-section goal design with proven actions we know work for us.

That's also an example of how our opinions of Personal Identities, like "*Crossfitter,*" create boundaries for us. I wanted to be an Athlete, and I wanted to use the Crossfit system to do it, but my safety mechanism told me I wasn't ready. It said I wasn't that *type of person*, and I believed it.

Thankfully I didn't sit idle while I was pausing and decided to prove I could change by exercising at home. I knew I could develop athletic skills with body-weight exercises like push-ups, squats, and burpees, and planned to do them while watching TV each night at home.

I had always been strong with push-ups in the past, so I decided to boost my self-esteem by starting with them. I figured they were my easiest skill to improve and would give me a quick win to feel great about myself. However, on day one, I had a big failure. I found I was much weaker than I thought and couldn't support my 285 pounds on my wrists and toes like normal.

The only way I could do a push up was by resting on my knees, which is the technique girls used in gym class at school. You can imagine that made me feel even more fat and depressed, but I told myself I had to fight through those feelings. Having that setback on day one was a big disappointment, but it was my fault for creating an *unproven expectation* of the actions I could take.

I had this idea of doing standard push-ups like I always had, because my opinion of my strength was tied to my performance when I weighed 175 pounds 20 years before. Of course I was upset when I couldn't do what I wanted, but I had to accept what I could do, at that time.

I had a real physical boundary that night, and no other choice but to start my recovery from there.

That meant accepting how out of shape I was, because that was the truth about my fitness. And I thought about quitting, like we all do, because my body and my pride were hurting. But my desire to change my P.I. to *Athlete* was stronger, and that wouldn't allow me to give up. I kept thinking about how good it felt to complete the obstacle race, and those memories reminded me of what I was working for, why it mattered so much, and how I could do it with a Changemaker mentality.

Since there was no other way to become who I wanted to be, I changed my exercise plan to fit my ability, and took my ego out of the equation. It didn't matter how strong I thought I was, or had been in the past, because on that first night I wasn't. So, I stopped being upset, and started doing the work that I could. I don't remember how many push-ups I did that night, or how long it took to get off my knees and back on my toes, but it was a great accomplishment when it happened.

What matters in this story is that I took charge of who I was, to become who I wanted to be. I ignored my fears, my ego, and my regret, and got to work doing the best I could at that time. Regardless of what my boundaries, opinions, or ego told me, I had to take the first steps of my thousand-mile journey on my knees.

Later that year I started training at a Crossfit gym, and in 2015 I competed in the Crossfit Open Games. I wasn't a ranked competitor, which are the people who really define the word Athlete, but that didn't matter to me. I had overcome the physical and mental boundaries I set out to in 2011, and my great accomplishment was knowing I would never again have to tell anyone that **"I'm just a Fat Guy, and we can't do that."**

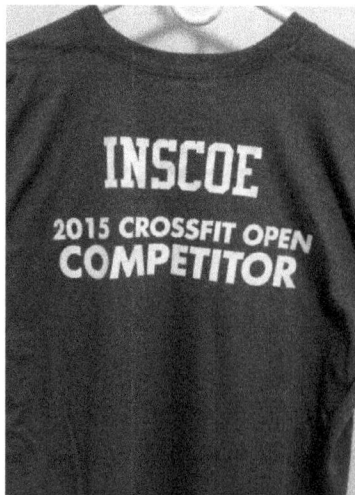

And that's how P.I. works for all of us. We must do the best we can when we start a new skill, or upgrade the ones we already have from where they are today. It isn't always fun, but it is always what we must do. Simple, not always easy.

Think of it like when a water pipe bursts in your home. It's upsetting, destructive, and inconvenient, but it's a real change you must deal with quickly. You can get mad and say you can't believe it's happening, but three things are undeniable:

1. The leak won't stop on its own, and your *opinion* won't change that.

2. Turning off the water supply, and ignoring the problem, isn't an option.

3. You need a qualified plumber to fix it, unless you have those skills in that moment.

That's why being a Changemaker is so important for creating and maintaining our Personal Identities to achieve new levels of success.

In the next chapter we're going to talk about our third Pillar of Success called F.U.D., which are our fears, uncertainties, and doubts. F.U.D. is the biggest obstacle we have for changing our P.I. but can become our most powerful tool for creating the successes we've been missing our whole lives.

CHAPTER 5

Pillar Three – F.U.D. - Fear, Uncertainty, and Doubt

Fear, Uncertainty, and Doubt (F.U.D.) is our third Pillar of Success. It's also the most powerful of the three, because the impact those thoughts, feelings, and emotions have in our life is bigger than our great accomplishments and P.I. combined.

In other words, F.U.D. is what keeps us from making the changes we need to succeed. To overcome its effects, we have to learn to recognize when they're happening, and know how to stop them.

No matter how clearly we define our great accomplishments, or how much we change our P.I. to earn them, F.U.D. can keep us from starting or finishing. That's because it feels normal to hold ourselves back and do less than we should. If we haven't succeeded with much in the past, it can be hard to believe we can change our lives on demand.

Whether it's *Three Pillars of Success,* or anything else, it might *sound* good at first, but when it's time to take action some of us will still be unsure it can work.

Changes and success can be scary, because people worry about what will happen if they try something new but fail. When those feelings come over us it's the ***signal*** to pay attention, because at those points we either don't get started, or we make smaller and safer changes to "*see what will happen.*"

That makes sense, because—until you're comfortable designing goals, managing changes, and feel your skills are an extension of you—transforming yourself can seem intimidating.

You might wonder:

> ➤ *What if something goes wrong?*

> ➤ *What would I do?*

> ➤ *How would I recover?*

That's how F.U.D. quietly influences us to think about less, do less, and accept less, while still convincing us that our less-risky actions are somehow successful. When it happens, it feels like our normal decision-making process, so we don't interpret it as a signal that change is needed.

Because we have this fear of "*doing too much,*" "*doing it too fast,*" or just plain failing, people often ask me "*What if I do this thing, and **It** doesn't work out?*" Since their skills aren't stronger yet, their feelings of F.U.D. take over and tell them the risk isn't something they should deal with.

My answer is always the same.

There is no "*It.*" There is only you.

When it comes to designing and creating success for ourselves, we think differently than we do about things we're already comfortable doing. The emotional stakes are higher, because we're not certain we can create what we want, or how to fix things if something goes wrong. That makes us think there are forces outside our control, and that "*It*" might not work.

But again, there is no "*It*," only your Great Accomplishments, Proven Actions, and Goal Designs.

So, when we start thinking in terms of "*It*," that's our signal that F.U.D. is saying we don't know enough about what we're doing and should stop. F.U.D. persuades us that the accomplishments we've already made are good enough, and it cautions us to avoiding making changes that could end in failure. F.U.D. tells us that we should put ourselves on pause without a plan, and safely enjoy what we already have.

But your current level of success isn't good enough, or you wouldn't be reading this book, right? That's a clear signal that we should ignore F.U.D. for a while and design some great accomplishments to get the results we want instead.

What's The Penalty? When I talk to people about F.U.D., I explain that if we don't look at the penalties we get for taking actions, having a setback, or failing completely, we're not seeing the most important part of the story. When little kids are learning to ride a bike, the penalty of falling isn't great enough to get them to stop. I've even seen a kid with his arm in a cast out there riding, because the worst part of that broken bone has passed, and he doesn't see a penalty to keep him from riding again.

But as adults, we talk ourselves into safety and out of success all the time. We also do it without any proof of what the penalty might be for trying and failing at something new, and we don't realize it's happening. So, as you read further, think about the idea that a penalty must outweigh the benefit of doing something new, and it must be a proven penalty to qualify. Otherwise, it's just F.U.D. telling you it's safer to not make changes and keep yourself on pause.

There's a famous story about Thomas Edison's journey to create the light bulb. It's believed he tried and failed with 9,999 designs before finding the correct solution on attempt number 10,000. It's obvious now he should have tried that hard to find the answer, but back then, there wasn't any proof that sustainable electric light was even possible. That didn't stop Edison though, and he never talked about *if* it would work, only what would happen *after it did*.

So, it's true you may fail with a Proven Action, or your entire goal many times, but that's how we learn to get better at the process of researching and designing. It's also how we eliminate resources in our goal designs that don't work for us, and figure out our limitations from category 1, 2, and 3 knowledge.

What it *never* means is that we are failures.

The timing may be wrong, our skills might not be strong enough yet, or variables we never knew about might get in our way. All that failure tells us is we didn't succeed within the schedule that we envisioned, or in the way that we planned, ***that time***. No big deal.

Failure is a tool we must learn from,
not a conclusion that tells us to stop.

At this point, I'm going to ask you to trust the process we're learning here and keep practicing until these tools and techniques become a part of you. That's the only way to feel like you own them and can use them to create the results you want. Our skills need to feel comfortable and obvious, like tying shoes or riding a bike, so practice is the only way to get there.

In this chapter, we're going to look at F.U.D. from three angles:

1. How F.U.D. got started in our lives.

2. How F.U.D. affects our accomplishments and goals.

3. How to transform F.U.D. into a tool for creating success.

Section 1 - How F.U.D. Got Started In Our Lives

To explain how F.U.D. affects our lives so deeply, we have to go back in time. Our feelings of F.U.D. work like instincts, dating back over 2 million years to when our ancestors lived in caves. Back then, F.U.D. played a bigger role in their lives because it had a very important purpose:

To keep them from getting killed.

Our ancestors needed that kind of help, because their brains weren't as developed as ours for making decisions to keep them safe. On top of that, they lived in a world with predators like saber-toothed tigers, so being cautious at all times helped them survive. And scientists say our feelings of F.U.D. most likely existed so we could live long enough to have children. We don't need that kind of help these days, but F.U.D. still regulates our lives as though we do.

It leads us to make safe (but irrational) decisions that don't require any critical thought. Neuroscientists call it the *"Caveman Brain,"* and even in the 21st century, and—as smart as we have become—we're still being controlled by the caveperson inside us.

And if our own irrational feelings weren't enough to keep us from succeeding, everyone we know shares their F.U.D. with us. We accept that help as part of our normal decision-making process, and we automatically know what to do because of our caveperson brain. It's like a shortcut to easily adopt their fearful experiences and become as safe as them. That means accepting smaller accomplishments and developing weaker P.I.'s and skills. All day long, our instincts tell us to avoid conflict, and listen to the experiences of others instead.

A common example of sharing F.U.D. is when someone tells you they had a bad experience at a restaurant. Some people will never go there as a result, even if the problem happened 3 years ago. Our instinct says it's safer to make choices we know the most about, so when we hear a bad review, we tend to believe it. We avoid places we only *heard* had a problem, without proving if it's true or not. The F.U.D. from others influences ours so quietly that even if the restaurant has a new owner and new food, some of us still won't go. We fail to realize that if there was a real problem, they would have either closed, or fixed the issue long before now.

When I was young, every adult of my parents' generation said that you couldn't go swimming right after you ate. No one knew what would happen to you, exactly, but that was the rule, and nobody broke it. Of course, it turns out that the warning is nothing more than superstition, and Science has long since debunked it.

But how many people of my generation still accept this as the truth? How many people have obeyed the no swimming after eating rule their entire lives, without ever seeking proof from a qualified resource? And how many parents are blindly passing this untruth on to future generations?

That's why we haven't been more successful in the past, because our F.U.D. influenced all the decisions we ever made. It makes you wonder how much of our lives are created by free will, and how much are the result of unproven fears that we accept from other people.

F.U.D. is the biggest reason American tourists look for American foods when they visit foreign countries. We believe that familiar choices are safer ones, regardless of where we are. But that's illogical, because food poisoning can happen inside a cheeseburger as easily as a roasted guinea pig or fried tarantula. It's not what you eat that causes the problem, it's how clean the kitchen is, and how safely the food was handled.

Regardless of logic or the facts, F.U.D. persuades us to choose familiar things because it's better to be safe than sorry.

Section 2 - How F.U.D. Affects Our Accomplishments, Goals, and Success

We were all born with F.U.D. instincts, and as kids they were influenced by the feelings of our parents and immediate family members. Their perceptions of the world automatically influenced ours, because it's normal for them to share, and for us to adopt the beliefs of our family.

At school our teachers and classmates shared their versions too, and if we went to a church or played on a sports team, we got a dose of F.U.D. there as well. All of this was completely normal, so no one ever thought to question the process. By the age of 20, we were pretty sure of what was safe for us, what to avoid, and how much success we *thought* a *person like us* could have.

Psychologists call that *Tribal Knowledge*, and though some of it is valuable, it automatically comes with a tone of F.U.D. Most cautionary tales or points of advice are delivered to us as established fact, without any proof, and without any expectations that we'll ask a question to verify it. After all, our tribe is made up of our family, friends, and the people we're closest to. Are normal thought is that whatever is good for one member of the tribe must be equally good for all.

Once again, it's the *Illusory Truth Effect* that we discussed in Chapter 3. Things sound more believable when they come from our closest advisors, which is why tribal knowledge has to be proven.

And even if you've never heard of the *Illusory Truth* before now, I'll bet you have experience with its cousin, *Common Sense*.

For a long time, people believed that everyone knew the same basics about living their lives. Those who had ideas that were different were thought to "*have something wrong with them*," because they weren't thinking and doing "*normal things*." Their ideas were seen as risky and scary, because no one in the tribe understood them, so they were immediately seen as wrong.

The concept of common sense in the U.S. goes back to our European ancestors who lived in villages, and farmed, traded, and worshipped together their whole lives. It's reasonable to say they had common knowledge about life in the village, because at the time, that was all you needed to know. Life was about survival, not individuality, and those ideals were brought to America with the Pilgrims in 1620.

And four hundred years later, people still believe that common sense is a reasonable and useful way to navigate through life. Putting your faith in something common feels safe, so people instinctively hang onto those beliefs as though they're established facts.

As an example, the F.U.D. I inherited from my tribe affected me deeply at the age of 15. That's when I decided to be an Entrepreneur, which went against the beliefs of my parents and everyone we knew. In the 1980's, having your own business or being an inventor was reserved for people who were personally accomplished, with money to protect them. But I came from a blue-collar family, where a job with benefits and a pension was the only common-sense thing to work for.

I had no support for anything outside of what my tribe said was safe, so I gave up on my own business and focused on school like I was told.

The F.U.D. my peers and I got from our tribal knowledge led us to think we had no ability to succeed in the ways that meant the most to us. "*Common Sense*" said that we shouldn't even try, which was backed up by the power of F.U.D. that everyone shared with us. Instead of creating great accomplishments, we followed the advice of the tribe, got a stable job they approved of, and put ourselves on pause without a plan.

Let Me Rephrase That: We put ourselves on pause by working in a job with a pension until the age of 65. That was the only acceptable plan in the past. We were only allowed to think about who we were and what we really wanted to do with ourselves "*later*," after a safe retirement.

But think about this regarding common sense:

> ➤ What if no one tried to make new discoveries?

> ➤ How would the world improve if no one took calculated risks?

> ➤ How do we know *we* aren't the ones who should be taking them?

What F.U.D. really tells us is to let others do the risk-taking, because it's safer to wait and see what happens than it is to take an action and fail. And that's what tribal knowledge and common sense have done to us, without ever looking like a signal to say we should change.

F.U.D. told us it was safer to be like everyone else, and up to now we either believed in that, or wondered what to do because we didn't know a better way. I say let's try something different, and *prove* which technique creates more success.

Section 3 - How To Transform F.U.D. Into A Tool For Success.

When we don't know what to do, by using logic and reason to find the answers, we're left with retreating to safety because of the caveperson inside us. And when I say retreat, I mean staying where we are and avoiding a change we're not sure we could ever make. That's why we need to learn a bit of our psychology to overcome what the caveperson says and start creating the successes we want.

When we have nothing else to believe in or make decisions with, F.U.D. automatically tells us who we are and what we can do. That's how F.U.D. is the biggest influencer of our Personal Identity, because it says we can't possibly be the type of person who accomplishes more. So, we stay who we think we are, put ourselves on pause, and accept that things are the way they're supposed to be.

"This is just who I am."

To hit the Play button, we have to do research to turn our Fears into **Facts**. At that point, our Uncertainty about the choices we can make becomes **Understanding** for what to do. And when you have facts and understanding on your side, Doubts turn into **Direction** for where you need to go, how to get there, and how long it will take.

- ➤ **F**ear becomes **F**acts.

- ➤ **U**ncertainty becomes **U**nderstanding.

- ➤ **D**oubt becomes **D**irection.

What we're doing here is transforming the old version of F.U.D. into the new, which is how it becomes a tool we create success with.

And to do that, there are only two things to recognize:

1. When F.U.D. is in charge, we automatically choose safety over success.

2. When F.U.D. shows up, that's our signal to create change, and get control over what we're afraid of.

How To Survive F.U.D.

The U.S. Army publishes a Survival Manual to teach soldiers for when they get lost or separated from their units. They need to know how to find food, water, and shelter, and lead themselves to safety while avoiding being captured. But survival is more than just the outward-facing techniques; it's really about dealing with F.U.D. That's why Chapter 2 of the manual introduces the psychology behind surviving, to explain how to deal with the stressors that affect our ability to make decisions.

It says: *"There is a psychology to **survival**. The **soldier** in a **survival** environment faces many stresses that ultimately impact on their mind. These stresses can produce thoughts and emotions that, if poorly understood, can transform a confident, well-trained **soldier** into an indecisive, ineffective individual with questionable ability to **survive**. Thus, every **soldier** must be aware of and be able to recognize those stresses commonly associated with **survival**."*

If we replace the word Survival with Success, and Soldier with Goal Designer, it reads lke this:

"There is a psychology to **Success**. The **Goal Designer** in a **Success** environment faces many stresses that ultimately impact on their mind. These stresses can produce thoughts and emotions that, if poorly understood, can transform a confident, well-trained **Goal Designer** into an indecisive, ineffective individual with questionable ability to **Succeed**. Thus, every **Goal Designer** must be aware of and be able to recognize those stresses commonly associated with **Success**."

Whether it's evading the enemy or telling ourselves we can design a goal to achieve a great accomplishment, the way that F.U.D. affects us is identical. So instead of giving into those feelings of fear, we need to do research to understand what they mean and what we can do about them.

That's why proving things is so powerful for us and is *required* to make the right decisions for our goals and great accomplishments. With research on our side, we learn the best way to deal with fearful subjects, if we should get help from coaches or mentors, and if we can avoid our feelings of F.U.D. altogether.

The best part of turning old F.U.D. into the new is that we'll quickly eliminate fearful things once we understand them. That means we either empower ourselves to deal with something we thought we never could, or we see how to ignore it and take a different route to achieve our great accomplishments.

Facing The Monster: When I was 12, I went on a class trip to an amusement park with a new roller coaster called The Loch Ness Monster. *"Nessie"* was taller, faster, and scarier than the others, which made it the highlight of the trip and the first thing my classmates wanted to do.

But I was scared.

I've always had a fear of heights, so my F.U.D. immediately told me to stay off the ride to be safe. And when I saw and heard the screaming riders as they flashed past us at 60 miles per hour, it reinforced how Nessie wasn't something I could do. In fact, I was more than just unsure about it, I had an irrational feeling that I wouldn't survive.

I don't mean a real fear of death, but that was the only way I could express what I was feeling. And as soon as I said to myself, *"I can't do that; I'll die,"* it became my reality.

That's how F.U.D. affects us so easily, by feeling like our normal decision-making process for things we don't understand and can't explain with words.

My F.U.D. was so strong it kept me from seeing or thinking about the facts:

1. Roller coasters are purpose-built machines designed to scare you.

2. Engineers build them from proven safety standards like cars.

3. In all the time I stood there, watching people get on and off, nobody was killed, or even injured.

But when we don't have facts to guide us, we irrationally think there's **no hope for us**. And we can't even use other people's good experiences to boost our confidence, because it's hard for those to overcome what our caveperson tells us. He/she creates our feelings without logic, reason, or the *use of language*, which is why we use the terms "*gut feeling*," or "*gut instinct*," to describe things we can't find the words for.

When we can't find the words to explain our fears, it's F.U.D. keeping us safe and the signal that we need to get the facts.

Later in the day I got a second chance to ride Nessie, because my classmates pressured me into doing it. I didn't have better facts by then, other than realizing no one had died all day, but I went. Peer-pressure is a very powerful influencer too, but earlier in the day it wasn't strong enough to overcome my F.U.D.

The first downhill drop on Nessie is 114 feet, which scared me in a way my caveperson did not like. But a moment later the speed, G-forces, and feeling of weightlessness in the corkscrew loops made it all worth it. It was an awesome experience for the 12-year-old me, because it was the most powerful ride I'd ever been on. It also proved to me how roller coasters weren't unsafe, and the penalty of the heights and downhill drops were far outweighed by the fun.

The ride lasted two minutes and ten seconds, which felt both like a lifetime, and the blink of an eye. And as soon as we finished, I wanted to go again.

I was hooked on the feelings of adrenaline, and I immediately had the facts I needed to overcome the F.U.D. that had kept me on pause all morning. I've been a fan of roller coasters ever since, even though I still have an irrational fear of heights. But because I've collected so many facts about my fear it can't control me in the way it used to. I make myself do things that are uncomfortable, and I research them to understand how safe they really are.

That gives me the power to do what I want by overcoming what the caveperson inside me will never stop saying. Once we practice turning fear into facts, we reignite the fire inside us we had to shut down so long ago. And when that happens, we're on the way to mastering our *Three Pillars of Success,* without the caveperson or anyone else controlling our path.

I Need To Quit My Job: My decision to quit my job, and work on *The Framework Life* project full time, is an example of transforming the old F.U.D. into the new.

My wife and I agreed I would publish the first book in the series, and make a certain amount of money, before leaving my career. But one Saturday I found myself at a crossroads where I couldn't "*see myself*" continuing to support my job and my project in the ways they needed. My P.I. had changed, and I knew that either my job or my project would suffer.

I also knew it was a signal that I needed to make a change.

I realized I was close to being published and had lost my tolerance for things at work that I didn't like and couldn't control. I was feeling emotionally done with my career, and ready to make the transition to full-time Entrepreneur. To figure things out, I had to get the facts on my side to understand what my choices really were.

My emotional self wanted to quit immediately because I was so frustrated, but my rational self knew that couldn't happen without money, and a proven plan for how to use it.

Right on schedule, three fears, uncertainties, and doubts entered my mind:

1. The first was that I would have to keep working while hating it, and not know how or when I could finish this book.

2. The second was that I had no idea how much money I had in savings, and how long I could go without making more.

3. The third fear was that my wife wouldn't understand how I felt, how quitting ahead of schedule was the key to my success and agree that I should do it.

My wife is more careful about taking risks, so I knew I needed a solid plan she could agree to. That meant maintaining the level of safety my income brought, and to figure that out I had to transform my F.U.D. into research I could make decisions with.

Solving that problem was easy, because all I needed was simple math. I had to figure out my monthly expenses, the total amount of cash and stocks I had, and determine how many months of freedom that would give me. In about 30 minutes I proved I had enough to live on for 18 months.

It's not that I expected to need that much time, but I needed to understand the worst-case scenario. Since being free to work for myself was my new great accomplishment, living off my savings account was the only way for me to do it.

Having the facts gave me the understanding of what my choices really were, compared to my emotional feelings of fear from earlier in the day. Before doing the math, I didn't know how much money I had to work with, and by looking at only my cash in savings I might have thought I wasn't ready. Failing to find all the information could have easily ended my plan for quitting my job and put my project at risk with uncertainties and doubts.

Simple research answered the first two of my fears with facts that proved to me how quitting my job was possible. But I also had to think six months into the future and estimate how much money I would lose by not working. Comparing that loss to the value of my freedom was another part of my proving process, to make sure I wasn't making an emotional decision that would cost me more than I knew.

Once I satisfied all my questions and had a proven plan to share with my wife, I felt ready to discuss it with her.

As expected, her immediate reactions were fear and confusion, because as far as she knew it was just another Saturday. Not only was she not expecting that discussion, my new proposal was the exact opposite of what we had agreed to long ago. In other words, I had abruptly removed the feelings of safety she had been comfortable in for years.

To restore that, remove her fears, and get her changemaker skills working with mine, I had to present facts she could agree with. Once I showed her how our financial safety wouldn't be changed by quitting my job, I proved to her that I had done the required work. And my plan was easy to understand, because it was based on simple math that anyone could agree with.

But when I said I had to quit my job; her immediate reaction was fear.

That's what happens to us when we're presented with a challenge, we don't understand or have the changemaker skills to deal with. The Navy SEALs specialize in managing unexpected changes, and we will succeed in bigger and faster ways by working like that too. Because F.U.D. exists to keep us choosing safe and familiar things, we need facts, experience, and our changemaker skills to overcome it.

> ➤ A barking dog sounds scary, until you see that she's playing with a ball.

> ➤ A man with a pistol on his belt looks scary, too, until you see he's a Police Detective.

> ➤ And quitting your job feels scary, until you know how much money you have, and how long it will support you.

Our feelings of fear, which are really the combination of Fear, Uncertainty, and Doubt, are a signal that change is needed.

Change means researching and proving what's really going on, so we can make the best decisions for completing our goals.

F.U.D. is a part of being human, and we can't turn that part of ourselves off yet. However, we can see those feelings as a signal, and be ready to transform them into **F**acts, **U**nderstanding, and **D**irection.

As soon as we do that, we have complete control over our *Three Pillars of Success*.

CHAPTER 6

Now and later Decisions

"I Don't Know What I'm Doing That Day"

I'm sure you've heard people say things like that when you invite them to something that will happen in the future. I've said it, and you probably have too, but did you ever wonder why we do it and what it means?

When people used to tell me, *"I can't think about that right now,"* or *"I don't know what I'm doing that day,"* it would really confuse me. Sometimes I would even get upset, because social plans are so easy to deal with. At least they are for me, so I couldn't understand why they were so hard for others. All it takes is a Yes or No, and we only need our calendar to help us figure it out.

In my mind it's just three simple decisions:

1. You're busy, or not.

2. You want to go to the event, or not.

3. You want to go with me, or not.

I figured people's lack of commitment was to leave their options open in case a better opportunity came up later; but I don't think that way anymore. It turns out we don't do these things on purpose, even though it can look like rudeness or indecision on the surface. But it's not either one of those things, and I don't think there's any conscious thought behind it at all.

Once again, it's our caveperson brain taking over our thoughts to maintain safety. We don't need that kind of help these days either, but it's still a part of our psychology we don't know how to turn off. That means we need to recognize when it happens and understand what it means to keep it from ruining our success.

In this chapter, we're going to learn more about how we make decisions, and how we can overcome the process to make faster and more successful ones the first time.

Our Brain Works Like A Computer: When we think about things to make decisions, our brain works like a computer processing data.

➤ Both need time to process.

➤ Both need fuel to process.

➤ Both *fail* when the process *overloads the system*.

Overloads are why people can't make a decision that seems sudden, complex, or too far in the future, like an invitation to a party that's three weeks away. Unless people know how to plan better and change faster, they get stuck trying to process and the idea gets shut down.

52

And these failures to process aren't consistent. They happen at different times, depending on the person and the topic they're trying to decide on.

Some people can make complicated decisions easily, others need extra time, and some can never "*get around to it.*" The challenge we all have is how much "*brain fuel*" we need to do the work. And that's not a phrase I invented; it comes from the study of Neuroscience. Brain fuel is the term scientists gave to the sugar called glucose, which is what our brain runs on.

Complex or unfamiliar ideas take more glucose/fuel to process and understand, and our caveperson's job is to protect us by conserving all that it can. He/she insists that we need all of ours to avoid danger and maintain safety, so we can't waste any on ideas that don't affect us ***Now***.

That's why some people's answers can't be Yes or No right away, and default to these:

➢ *I don't know what I'm doing then/that day/that weekend.*

➢ *I don't know, ask me in three months.*

➢ *I don't know, I can't think about that right now.*

In other words, "**Go away, your questions cost too much to think about**."

This behavior comes from another part of our psychology we're not aware of, and it makes us put information into three categories:

➢ *Now or Later.*

➢ *Concrete or Abstract.*

➢ *Safe or Unsafe.*

Now ideas are so familiar that we can deal with them immediately. They're also called *concrete*, because we have a solid understanding of what they are, what they mean to us, and how to deal with them. That means they're *safe* to deal with, because the amount of brain fuel they cost to process won't put us in danger.

Talking to your coworkers about lunch is a common *Now* idea that most everyone can deal with. We know lunch is at noon, we like eating with coworkers, and it's a "*problem*" we're accomplished at solving. We also know the ten restaurants we always go to, so if the pizza shop is crowded, we easily move on to our next familiar choice without expending too much effort.

But if you try to schedule a pizza lunch date for 45 days from now, some people will tell you they can't think about lunch that far out. Even ideas as safe and concrete as lunch and pizza become hard to think about when you add the abstract concept of *time*. Planning that far ahead is scary for some, and their caveperson tells them it's unsafe to burn more fuel to figure it out. We need to reserve all we can for making *Now* decisions, and we certainly can't afford to use today's fuel allowance to solve a problem that's in the future.

Without realizing it we think things like:

> ➤ *"Will I be at work that day?"*

> ➤ *"What happens if I don't want pizza then?"*

> ➤ *"What could get in the way between now and then, and turn this decision into a* ***disaster****?"*

To me, it's easy. I could schedule a pizza lunch with you for five years from now without a second thought. I know there's no penalty for doing it, and I know how to deal with anything that might keep us from meeting. But to others, even a casual social commitment set so far in the future requires a painful set of decisions they just can't handle. The caveperson won't allow it, so they have to push the request away to maintain their feelings of safety.

Talk To You Later: Future concepts, like lunch in 45 days, are classified as *Later* ideas in our brain, and they require long-term thinking that we aren't good at dealing with. They're considered abstract because they're not clearly defined, and we don't have enough experience in handling them. They use too much fuel to think about, for a future *that may never come.* That's why our caveperson doesn't want us to process them.

Real cave people had to survive from day-to-day without any feeling that they could control the outcome. That instinct is still inside us and says we may starve and die if we don't conserve brain fuel *now.* As a result, we say things like *"let's wait and see what happens,"* when we don't know how to deal with something that seems too abstract or hard to understand. When ideas *"cost too much"* to think about, it feels like we can't *"afford"* to deal with them *now,* so we don't.

And these *later* and *long-term* ideas don't even have to be a long time from now, which is the worst part of this.

A *later* idea could be a party in three days, graduating from college in four years, or any time in between. All that matters is whether we think the ideas are too hard to deal with *at this moment.* Once our caveperson brain decides that an idea or question costs too much fuel to process, we stop working on it and try to postpone the decision indefinitely. Our caveperson secretly hopes that the matter won't ever come up again, and that he/she will *never* have to use the fuel to cope with it.

Think about all the people who take a *"Gap Year"* off between high school and college, or between undergraduate and graduate school. I don't how many of those people actually return to complete their education, but—from what I've heard and seen—I don't think the percentage is high.

The idea of returning to school can be overwhelming for many people, because they either have no great accomplishment driving them to do it, or because F.U.D. tells them they're not good enough to succeed. So, they use the technique of the gap year to give them time to decide *"later,"* which often means hoping that time never comes.

It's hard for many people to process abstract thoughts and feelings, and even harder to determine if they'll ever need those abstractions in order to succeed. Thinking about *later* ideas actually creates painful and anxious feelings for some. Their heads physically hurt when they have to burn more fuel to think through abstract concepts, so it's easier for them and their caveperson to halt the process instead.

But by understanding what's going on, and practicing researching to get the facts, we can rewire our brains to work through that difficulty.

Short-term and Long-term Goals: I grew up hearing those terms as a kid, but never got a clear lesson on how to use them. I didn't know if short- and long-term could help us create greater success, and I didn't know anyone who knew the answer. I lived for decades without giving the matter serious thought, and my caveperson was happy that I wasn't using extra fuel to figure it out.

But as the concepts around Three Pillars began to evolve in my mind, I decided I had to know. So, I overrode my caveperson and burned that extra fuel.

What I found is that we use the terms short-term and long-term as comfort words, to feel like we're organized and in control of our goals. Putting goals into categories feels like the normal thing to do for many people, but I can't find any evidence that it helps us create bigger levels of success or do it more quickly.

Instead of empowering us, these commonly-accepted categories actually hold us back:

1. They make us focus on things we *think* we can do *now*.
2. They push away ideas we don't understand and classify them as *later*.

That's how the caveperson maintains safety, and why it's hard for us to see when it happens.

If you already knew how to design and schedule goals for great accomplishments, calling them short or long-term wouldn't get in your way. They would just be labels in that case, and no different than saying "*I have a fun goal, and a serious goal.*" When you know what you're doing you can call them anything you like without it changing how you think or take action.

But when you don't have those skills, labels not only *don't add value* but keep you from achieving greater success. What they actually do is help you classify things more quickly as *now* or *later* ideas. Short-term and long-term labels create another illusion we learned from Tribal Knowledge, but their only purpose is to lead us toward safety; not success.

How Long Is Short? If we think short-term means six months or less, but can't get organized to succeed in that time, what happens? Some people will change the label to long-term and keep working, but most people will feel some F.U.D. and start thinking they can't do it. Failing with something that we've identified as short-term feels like failing with something clear, concrete, and attainable. When we can't figure it out, it damages our P.I. and makes us feel like we're not the *type of person* we thought we were.

As soon as F.U.D. tells us that's not *who we are*, we believe that's *not the goal we can accomplish,* and we stop trying. Some people are strong enough to try again, but most of us will put ourselves on pause to see how we feel *later*. But later doesn't exist on any calendar and waiting won't help us find it.

If we do set goals again, we'll do it in a loop of classifying them as short- or long-term, safe or unsafe, *now* or *later*. The "*Nows*" we'll do now, the "*Laters*" we'll *say* we're going to get to, and the caveperson will succeed by conserving as much fuel as possible.

Short-Term Doesn't Mean Successful: The goals we think we can accomplish *now* aren't pushing us to find and exceed our personal bests. Even if we think they're great accomplishments, that's only in the context of what we believe we are capable of *right now*. It's another P.I. boundary that says to dial back our expectations of how far we can go.

The idea of transforming our lives is about discovering how *great* our great accomplishments can be, every time we try. It's like hitting a Personal Record (PR) in the gym, where we continue improving our skills to hit the next one and see how far our "*far*" can be. Labeling goals as short-term doesn't push us to do that, and instead sabotages the process of expanding our goals. It makes us focus on the clear, concrete, and *now* ideas that feel safer, while delaying everything else until *later*.

The questions we need to answer are not what *short-term* and *long-term* mean, but why we think we need labels, and what really happens when we accept and use them.

Labels are why so many goals never get started, finished, or designed to reach our personal bests because we're never allowed to use the fuel to figure them out. We also don't realize we're being held back, because if it's not short-term then it must be long, and we're sure we'll get to it *later*.

The *Illusory Truth* tells us that everything is okay, because we're setting goals and creating accomplishments. In reality, we're pausing without a plan on ideas we don't know how to deal with, to buy ourselves time to figure them out. But by labeling them long-term, we don't have to think about them *now*, which too often means that we'll never find the time.

In Chapter 3, we established that success is created from goals that achieve great accomplishments. I didn't say we needed categories to help us, and now you see why they're actually damaging to our success. Categories only benefit the caveperson by conserving our brain fuel and trying to create safety.

In Chapter 8 we're going to learn more about goal design, to avoid thinking that *later* and *long-term* have anything to do with being successful.

If You Can't Decide, It's A SIGNAL: When we catch ourselves putting off a task, pushing away things we don't understand, or thinking we're too busy to deal with them, that's our *signal* to stop and remember this concept. Those feelings tell us that we're dealing with abstract, unclear, and *later* ideas, which is when we need to *get curious*.

We need to clarify all ideas to see if they could be a resource to us, and the fact that we want to push them away says we should actually pull them closer. Think back to what we said about resources in Chapter 3. We need to decide if information and people can help us, understand how they can, and determine for how long. But all of that gets lost when we allow the caveperson to shut down our thought processes and convince us to avoid thinking through unclear things.

So, think of this like swallowing cough syrup. Most of them taste terrible, but we take them anyway because they contain the medicine we need. To succeed more now, and into the future,

I'm asking you to treat information you don't want to deal with like cough syrup. If you keep dismissing abstract, unclear, and *later* information without researching the value, you'll always miss the medicine inside without ever being aware of what you've lost.

Don't push ideas away.

Push through them to find the facts.

This is another skill we need to practice, and the better we get at thinking and analyzing, the faster and more efficient we'll become at making successful decisions. With practice, abstract thinking won't always hurt your head, and when it does, you'll know that the brain fuel you're burning is actually a good investment.

At this point, I can almost hear some of you saying this, "*not every social invitation is critical to our success.*" No, it's not. However, the skill of evaluating information we don't want to deal with *is* critical. Since we know it takes more brain fuel to process the things we "*can't think about right now,*" we have to remember how easy it is to push them away and never come back to them. In the past, we missed the signals to investigate the value of information, and we've got fewer skills, accomplishments, and less money because of it.

We've also lost time that we can't get back, where we should have been practicing the evaluation of abstract ideas. But we know better now, which means we can change all that starting today.

When I was in my 20's and 30's I didn't learn what I should have about investing in my 401k for retirement. I contributed less than I should for 15 years and missed out on making money that compound interest would have created. I can never get that chance again, because those years can't be repeated.

I always told myself I would learn more about investing *later,* but never defined when that time was. Thinking about it back then hurt my head, because it was hard to understand and cost too much fuel to process. So, I pushed it into the future without making a plan with a date to get started. I learned the hard way it's smarter to pause for a moment, write down what you need to research, and prove whether those *later* ideas could be a resource to you *now*.

Otherwise, it's easy to dismiss something that could become a great accomplishment, help us avoid a P.I. boundary, or turn F.UD. into a tool to help us succeed. When we don't get curious about things, people, and ideas, we aren't practicing our thinking, designing, and Changemaker skills. So, until you get better at making faster and more accurate decisions, you have to keep asking yourself "*How Do I Know,*" and making the time to prove those answers to yourself.

You don't have to go fast when you do it, but you do have to practice until it feels normal.

For me it's easy to make notes and reminders, and every smartphone has apps that can help you. If you have a phone, you have the exact tool you need right now.

Thomas Edison had a harder time dealing with abstract ideas and needed paper notebooks to keep track of all the materials he tested to make the sustainable light bulb. I'm glad he was so thorough, because we've lived our entire lives within the light of his dedication.

But imagine how different our world would be if Edison had allowed himself to be overwhelmed by the abstract and unclear information he had to work through. And imagine if he said to himself:

"I don't know if this is possible,
and I can't think about it right now."

CHAPTER 7

What You Say Determines Where You Go.

There's an old expression... "*It's not what you say, it's how you say it.*"

I think we all heard that one growing up, and it's true that *how* you say things to people makes a difference. We all respond to different styles of language, and when people speak to us in ways that we don't like or understand, it changes how we feel about the message, and them.

If great news is given to us in the wrong way, it can ruin the moment, just like bad news can be shared with language that softens the impact.

But isn't it also true that what we say and how we say it, *to ourselves,* changes how we feel about *who we are* and *what we can do*? It certainly is true, because language is the tool we use to create our Personal Identity. Whether we say it out loud or not, we can talk ourselves into (or out of) doing anything, and we always have.

The question we need to answer now is:

Have I been talking about the right things?

The focus of this chapter is understanding how powerful our use of language is, and how we can create both positive and negative results with what we say to ourselves. Using language in the right way is a vital tool for our goal design process, to make each goal as powerful as possible the first time.

What you say determines where you go is one of my favorite quotes because it's completely true. We need to keep that concept in mind while we're thinking, designing, and changing, because what we say about ourselves determines the actions we will take.

And the power of language works like this:

> ➢ Words *create* or *deflate* our great accomplishments.

> ➢ Personal Identity is a *picture* in our mind we paint with words.

> ➢ Disempowering words, and *qualifiers,* come from F.U.D., and put us on pause without a plan when we don't realize what we're saying.

Words that diminish us, like *dumb, stupid,* and *hopeless* are obvious, and need to be removed from our vocabulary. But *qualifiers* are different and—in their own way—even more dangerous. Because they're so harmless sounding they go unnoticed, which quietly reinforces in our minds that they're true.

Qualifiers are words that dilute the meaning of action statements and deflate our ability to create success. I say deflate, because we can't design goals to achieve great accomplishments by using insecure language that doesn't drive us to concrete actions and results. Everyone knows you can't get a little bit pregnant, but we keep using qualifiers when talking about success.

> ➤ I'm *kinda* doing my own business.

> ➤ I'm *sorta like* an Entrepreneur.

> ➤ I'm *trying* to make some changes.

Kinda, sorta like, and trying aren't direct and purposeful, and if you think about the people you call successful, they didn't get there using language like that. Qualifiers soften our message in a way that says we aren't committed because we don't feel in control.

That's another way P.I. boundaries are created, that say we're not good enough to go further, and should stay right where we are. Once again, it's the caveperson and F.U.D. giving us a path back to safety, so we have to fight against those feelings by researching the facts.

If I say I'm *"kinda"* doing my own business, it tells everyone I'm not serious. We all understand that I'm simply trying it out to see what will happen and hoping for the best. *"Kinda"* is how we prepare others to agree that it's okay if *"It"* doesn't work out, and when we fail no one will be shocked.

What it should tell us is we don't have enough facts and need to do more research.

We grew up learning to praise ourselves and others for simply *trying* things that were risky, and that legitimized failure as ***the normal and expected outcome***. We were never taught to expect or design success, so nobody holds us to a higher standard. Qualifiers allow us to support each others' failures more easily and add them to our tribal F.U.D. to keep each other safe. Qualifiers are also how we easily put ourselves on pause without a plan, in a way that others won't question.

And then there's the ***King of all Qualifiers***: The word "***Just***."

By definition Just means many things, but the version we're talking about here means *"only,"* or *"simply."*

"I just want a cup of coffee" means I simply want, or only want a cup of coffee. That would be the correct use of the word if you already ate breakfast and didn't wish to eat with me now.

But that's not how we use it most often, which is the reason it's so dangerous to us.

> ➤ *I'm just asking.*

> ➤ *I'm just wondering.*

> ➤ *I'm just hoping.*

In other words: *"I'm just using a qualifier, because softening everything feels easier and less threatening when I'm not confident and just trying something out to see if **It** will work."*

Think about the qualifiers you've been using, and how they sound to you now. If you don't listen to how you speak to yourself and others, you'll miss those signals and keep deflating your ability to create great accomplishments.

When we use the word "*Just*," what we're actually doing is asking for relief. We're frustrated or scared by our circumstances, and we don't feel enough control.

> ➢ *I just want a break*

> ➢ *I just want to go home.*

> ➢ *I just wish life wasn't so hard.*

Like all qualifiers, "*Just*" is a sign that F.U.D. is telling us to think about less, do less, and accept less. That's our signal to figure out what our fear is, so we can find the facts and get empowered.

I said in Chapter 4 that our P.I. tells us who we think we are, which tells us what we think we can do. Then I said to change our P.I. we need to envision the type of person we need to be and get the skills they have to become that type. But I didn't describe the best way to do it, which is to change the way we think about and talk to ourselves, because what we say determines where we go.

All our lives, we've been using language in the wrong way, or at least in a way that hasn't helped us achieve the levels of success we want. Today is the time to choose empowering words that create those results, while removing the qualifiers that have limited us so much in the past.

He Started Over At 52: If you don't know the name Ray Kroc I wouldn't be surprised, but I'll bet you know his work very well. Kroc is the founder of McDonald's restaurants, which he didn't get involved with until the age of 52. When most people were thinking about their retirement years, Ray Kroc was just getting started.

For the 15 years before that, he was selling milkshake mixing machines used by restaurants. But by the 1950's the economy was changing, and people were leaving big cities to start new lives in the growing suburbs. The restaurants that bought shake mixers were closing, and Kroc's business was in dissolving before his eyes.

Instead of retreating to another sales job, he turned his fears into facts to figure out how he could succeed next. One of his largest customers, the McDonald brothers of San Bernardino California, had a restaurant model Kroc had never seen before. He liked it so much he offered to franchise their ideas exclusively, and the brothers agreed.

In his autobiography, "*Grinding It Out*," Kroc says his great accomplishment had been to sell a milkshake mixer to every place that needed one in the U.S. But that changed the day he met the McDonald brothers, and saw how they ran their simple burger, fry, and milkshake stand.

Kroc had a vision for how that concept could be popular everywhere, so he reinvented himself and got started. Franchising is common these days, but back then it was not a widely accepted business model. Kroc had to convince the McDonald brothers that it was a good idea for them.

In his first year, he opened 18 locations, which didn't make as much money as he planned. His financial model was wrong, so he redesigned it to buy or lease the land the franchised stores were built on. That gave him an additional stream of income that was guaranteed, beyond just a percentage of the food sales. Setbacks and failures weren't a sign for him to stop; they were a signal that change was needed *now*.

Seven years later, in 1961, Kroc bought the business from the McDonald brothers and became the sole owner. He was 59 years old and getting started once again on a bigger set of great accomplishments. Over the next four years he opened 700 McDonald's restaurants in the U.S., and that number rose to nearly 1,500 around the world by 1970.

In sixteen years, he had created the largest restaurant franchise in the world, which is still the case today with $89 billion in sales in 2018. When people would ask Kroc "*What does it take to get a McDonald's franchise?*" his answer was simple:

> *"A total commitment of personal time and energy is the most important thing. A person doesn't need to be super smart or have more than a high school education, but he or she must be willing to work hard and concentrate exclusively on the challenge of operating that store."*

People say you have to be really smart and maybe a little gifted to create results like Kroc's, and that may be true. But what is 100% true is that success at *any* level is a result of how you talk to yourself about your goals.

Nobody "*kinda succeeds,*" and you can't create specific results by saying "*I'm gonna try,*" or "*we'll see what happens.*" It's always F.U.D. that makes us think and talk like that, and we can't allow those thoughts, feelings, and emotions to tell us what we can do. When we can't clearly explain what we're doing, and why, it's our signal that F.U.D. has taken control. It's also the signal that we need to get **curious** and investigate those fears to uncover the facts.

I Think It's Too Soon: In Chapter 4, I talked about wanting to go to a Crossfit gym after my obstacle race in 2011. But I didn't do it right away. After the excitement of the race was over, my Personal Identity was still too weak and my F.U.D. kept me on pause. I was afraid it was "*too soon*" for the gym because I was so fat and out of shape. I hadn't done any research to understand the facts about Crossfit, and instead was using my *opinion* of the facts. Fear made me unsure I could keep up with those "*real athletes,*" and because of that I doubted whether it was the right choice for me at all.

Because of the people I saw at my race, I made up a story in my mind that Crossfit was like the military. I told myself I had to become faster, stronger, and more capable before I could join up. But I had no idea how to achieve those levels of personal improvement, so my desire was quickly becoming a *later* idea. I started pushing it away, because the anxiety of not having control over myself was too much.

Thankfully, a coach from the gym I wanted to go to worked in my office and told me how all the exercises were designed to be tailored for anyone's fitness level. That was a relief because this guy was lean, athletic, and muscular, which only reinforced how unqualified I was to join the gym.

Eventually I asked him questions about how Crossfit could work for me, and he invited me to watch a class he was coaching at lunchtime. As soon as I saw how the process worked, all my fears **disappeared**. One conversation, and one 30-minute visit was all it took to understand how I could design my fitness goals to take action immediately.

It was like the lights were turned on, and I could see all the facts about my fears that had put me on pause without a plan.

Before that moment, though, I was sure I wasn't capable of doing Crossfit. My F.U.D. had me convinced that *"you're still a Fat Guy, and it's too soon,"* and I agreed with it.

I Think I've Done Enough: Like other sports, achieving a performance goal in Crossfit is called hitting a Personal Record. We call it a PR for short and reaching and exceeding those is our focus. In fact, hitting PR's is what athletes do in every sport, and is the perfect example of having a great accomplishment as the outcome of your goal design

But that was a lesson I had to learn the hard way. I never told myself I *couldn't* do something at the gym, but I did believe I knew when I had *"done enough"* and should stop. That's not how fitness, or any goal works, and when we talk to ourselves that way it's actually F.U.D telling us what to do.

Without better information to guide us, it's easy to believe that we need to slow down. With no conscious decision, we start talking ourselves into smaller accomplishments in all areas of our lives. We get comfortable with *"an accomplishment,"* instead of working toward PR's that are structured like a goal to achieve a great one.

When I deadlifted 315 pounds, that's exactly what happened. 315 was a PR I didn't know I could reach, but my coach told me to keep working toward it. To me it sounded like *"a really heavy weight,"* and the most I could ever possibly lift. I had no experience or proof to back that up, but F.U.D. told me it was my reality.

The biggest reason I thought that way was my technique was wrong, and I didn't know it. I was using brute force to get the weights off the floor, which caused unnecessary joint and muscle pain. The right technique would have avoided that, but I didn't realize I needed help.

The night I finally hit that PR felt amazing, but it hurt more than it should have. No matter, I celebrated because I was convinced I would never have to do it again. My coach saw what I was doing, and said *"great job, but you know you can do more, right?"*

"Did she say <u>more</u>?"

I had worked really hard and felt I had done the most my body could handle. Being told to do *more* sounded like criticism and made me a little defensive. Being challenged sent my F.U.D. into overload, because more weight only meant more pain and suffering. To protect me, my F.U.D. jumped in and told me to say this:

"But I just hit a PR; I can't lift more weight!"

Like a child arguing with a teacher, I tried to explain how more wasn't possible. I was the student, and she was the Olympic Weightlifting Coach, but that's how F.U.D. works when we don't understand the facts. Instead of getting **curious** about what's going on, we tell ourselves what we can and cannot do and use irrational statements to push people away in the name of safety.

Later I learned she wasn't criticizing me at all but encouraging me to keep achieving new levels of strength. I also learned I needed to correct my technique, so I could safely lift more. But the most important lesson was that I had to talk to myself differently to achieve that goal.

In Crossfit, every PR is a great accomplishment. Sometimes you need help from the coaches to improve your technique and discover what your physical limits really are to get there. That's what coaches are for, to show you the path to go further. But when you don't ask for help, you'll struggle, and convince yourself of this: "*I Think I've Done Enough.*"

As soon as we say that, it becomes our reality and we're done.

What we say to ourselves truly determines where we go in all parts of our lives, so we can't afford to tell ourselves a story that isn't proven by facts. Instead, we have to focus on thinking about great accomplishments to drive our thoughts and actions. The best part of talking positively to ourselves is we will maximize successes in new chapters of our lives, or with old goals that we didn't succeed with and want to redesign.

Ray Kroc redesigned his life at the age of 52, which tells me the game isn't over until we decide to stop playing. He retired from McDonald's at the age of 72 but wasn't finished working or reinventing himself. His next idea was to buy the San Diego Padres baseball team and take them to the World Series. The man never stopped working because he loved what he did so much that it never felt like work at all.

When we look at his career, it's nothing but impressive. He repeatedly recreated his Personal Identity and redesigned his goals, and we can only guess how much F.U.D. he overcame to do that. His journey shows how powerful our language is for driving us to success, and how age doesn't matter once we tell ourselves exactly what we want to do.

The world was much more conservative between 1950 and 1970, and risk wasn't understood or comfortable for most. Money and credit were harder to get, and if you didn't have experience in an industry like food sales or real estate, people thought you weren't qualified to do business with.

The challenges we have today are easier compared to what people like Kroc dealt with their whole lives. And yet here we are, telling ourselves we can't do something because we never have, or because we can't immediately envision a path to success.

The answer is simple with *Three Pillars of Success*, once we use empowering language that says, "*this is who I am, and this is what I'm doing.*"

But What About… When I talk to people about this topic of language, they sometimes bring up an exception that F.U.D. tells them can't possibly work. They say things like "*but what about X, Y, or Z? How is that going to work by talking to myself?*"

Of course, it can't at that point, because the very words they've chosen show that they've surrendered to F.U.D. By using doubtful language, they've put the caveperson in charge of the brain fuel for making more complex decisions. They didn't see those feelings as a signal to research their fears, and they gave away their vote by getting safely put on pause.

If you're looking for a reason to stop, F.U.D. and the Caveperson will help you every time.

On the other hand, if you're looking for a way to succeed, tell yourself what you are going to do, design a plan, and research to find the facts that you need.

Stopping when F.U.D. tells us to is not our fault, because we've been doing these things instinctively our whole lives. We've practiced fear and failure techniques because safety feels better than risk when you're not trained to ask, "*how do I know*," and research the facts. No big deal though, because now that we know what's happening, we're going to practice changing what we say to ourselves. And when we do, it will immediately change our results.

To finish up this topic, I want to show you some examples of what it sounds like when we talk ourselves out of success, and into the arms of safety. I've heard this kind of "*Failure Talk*" my whole life, without understanding what it really meant and how it's created by our caveperson and F.U.D. in the blink of an eye.

"I just want to be happy."

People who have never been successful think you have to choose between success and happiness. Their Tribal Knowledge, Common Sense, and F.U.D. have convinced them that's how it works, and the biggest cause behind it is the idea that money is the official measure of success.

When we believe that being successful means having "*a lot of money*," and we don't know how to earn more than we do today, success feels like a place *we* could never get to. In fact, success is so complicated and painful for some of us to think about the caveperson shuts the process down to conserve brain fuel. We push the idea off until "*later*," which really means never, and try to make our lives "*as happy as they can be."*

But what is the measurement for "*as happy as they can be*," and how do we know when we've gotten there?

Every time someone has told me they "*just want to be happy*," it sounded like a plea for help. And again, the word "*Just*" tells us how tired they are of struggling. They say they want to be happy, but they aren't even sure what that means or how to achieve it. I asked someone why they weren't happy by now, and they gave me a list of things they had to do first. They couldn't even "*see themselves*" being happy in that moment, because their lives and the world around them were so overwhelming.

At the time I didn't know it, but the questions we have to ask in that case are:

1. How do you know you can't make more money using the skills you love, and get paid well for it?

2. How do you know you can't start now, and improve those skills every day, week, and month?

3. Where is the proof that your life has been decided without your permission, and your only hope is to be as happy as you can be with whatever you're given?

Being as happy as you can be sounds like a prison sentence to me, but it can all change with what we say to ourselves while we're building our *Three Pillars of Success.*

"I don't need a lot of money to be happy."

This is a variation on *"I just want to be happy,"* except now they're defending the idea that making less money than they could or being underpaid for their time, is acceptable.

I always ask them two questions:

1. How do you know if you've never had *"a lot of money?"*

2. How many dollars are there in *"a lot of money?"*

Those aren't fair questions, because I know they have no idea how to answer either one. For some reason, people think money changes you into a *"bad person,"* or as I said earlier, they can't imagine how to earn what they think of as a lot of it. To stop the pain of thinking through something so difficult, they have to create an excuse for their behaviors.

Making yourself happy by accepting whatever you have is the common one. In Psychology, that's called **Rationalizing**. It means to think and talk about an irrational idea as though it's normal and acceptable. An example is an obese person telling their Doctor they *feel healthier* that way, and don't need to lose weight. It's also like a poor person telling you that more money would *"just make them miserable,"* or *"just cause more problems."*

Once again, that's F.U.D. telling you not to take any risks, and that you're not good enough to succeed if you did. To be safe, you should stay who you are, don't get the skills that make more money, and create a story that you try to make believable. That's what being on pause without a plan is about too, and some people do that their whole lives.

But you don't have to live that way, and you don't have to be pressured into making a lot of money doing something that isn't a great accomplishment for you. However, believing that you're happier being poor and struggling is not healthy, and rationalizing is a skill that only gives F.U.D. more control.

"Good things come to those who wait."

This is an old saying that has been disproven countless times, usually by the same people who cling to it. If it were true that all we need to do is wait for success to find us, we would see the evidence of our older friends and relatives prospering by now. But that's not what happens, and since waiting is not a skill, we can't practice it to create positive results.

You could argue that waiting is just having patience, but without a design to guide us, and a schedule for when to take proven actions, we won't know when to get ourselves off pause.

In my experience this phrase comes from a time when it was *common sense* that you couldn't change your life on demand. From the 1950's to the early 2000's, people didn't have information and opportunities to get or upgrade skills very easily, so hard work and patience were all anyone knew for two generations. The belief was that if you became good at your job you might eventually get promoted, but you had to wait until someone retired or transferred to open up that spot.

We don't have to wait for skills and opportunities like that these days, and I'll bet you can't think of one example where not getting skills, not making a plan, and not taking proven actions made anyone more successful.

Unfortunately, many people still believe in waiting for good things to "*come along,*" because it costs too much brain fuel to work through the ideas of what we should be doing. That's why people love this next statement, because when you don't have the tools and techniques to succeed, this explains why it's not your fault and why you don't have to worry.

"Everything happens for a reason."

This statement has so much power over us *because it's absolutely true*. You either create results with your actions, or someone (or something) creates results without you.

That's the "*reason*" everyone is talking about, though people usually think it means that some higher power is making sure that everything works out for the best.

To make the reality of their F.U.D. and failures more bearable, people create these irrational statements to comfort themselves:

➤ If the bakery is out of your favorite muffin it just means you should start your diet, because *everything happens for a reason.*

➤ If you haven't met the love of your life it just means your soul mate is still looking for you, because *everything happens for a reason.*

➤ And if you don't get that job or promotion you wanted it just means something even better is coming, because *everything happens for a reason.*

The Truth Is This: If your career sucks, you're underpaid, got the wrong degree in college, can't get a better job, and have no idea what you're doing, it actually means *you have no idea what you're doing.*

And again, that's not an insult, it's the report card that tells us we need to start making changes. There is no Fate, Karma, or Destiny working for us in the background, so it's up to us to create the changes we need. Psychologists say when we try to convince ourselves that things happen for a reason, it's because we need to believe that we're being protected by a higher power. They go on to say it's really a combination of our fear, anxiety, and anger that makes us think this way. We're afraid of our problems, we don't know how to handle them, and we're angry that we're afraid and don't know what to do.

Worse than that, our brains are continually looking for patterns to help make sense out of random occurrences. When we're failing at things, and don't know how to succeed, F.U.D. tells us there *MUST* be a reason that we can believe in. It's driven by the same pattern matching process that makes us see faces, or horses, or dinosaurs in the shapes of the clouds

In the absence of a valid pattern, our caveperson brain invents one to keep us from burning fuel to figure out what we're actually seeing.

That's the definition of rationalization; generating a believable pattern out of data points that either don't go together, or don't even exist. It's also how F.U.D. comes to our rescue to explain that *none of this is our fault*. But thinking that way can't create success in our lives, so what we need are the right thoughts and words to lead us to proven actions.

Believing there's a force outside our control only takes our choice-making away. Then it puts us on pause without a plan to take the pressure away from being fearful, unsure, or doubtful.

That's why so many people love to say these phrases to each other, because it brings them comfort.

But once again, it's the *Illusory Truth Effect*, where we believe unproven things because we hear them often, from a broad range of sources, and specifically from our closest friends and relatives. You see this over and over on social media, where a popular misunderstanding of something becomes viral because people desperately want to believe it.

The old saying about birds of a feather flocking together is true, and their levels of success are determined by the things they say and believe.

When your F.U.D. says goals and success only mean risk and failure, you'll stay where you are and rationalize that things happen outside your control. And it's comforting to imagine that things happen for the *right reasons*, when in reality it's another signal that change is desperately needed.

So, the next time you feel like your successes are influenced by outside forces, stop and remind yourself of this:

Everything happens for a reason,
and the reason is me.

In the next chapter, we're going to talk about organizing our limited resources to design our goals for the biggest results we can create, at the fastest speeds. When we do that, everything will happen for a reason that we designed, and no amount of F.U.D. can ever change that.

CHAPTER 8

Designing Goals with Gap Analysis & RDOM2

In Chapter 3, we talked about designing goals versus setting them, and I said we would discuss that more in detail. Before we do, though, I want to explain where the concept of goal design came from, and why it's such a powerful tool for us.

I worked in the IT industry for nearly 22 years, on many successful project teams. I say successful, because the network systems we built or upgraded always worked in the way the projects required. We had setbacks like everyone does, but in all those years we never failed, and we never said the work couldn't be done. We also didn't think our successes were unique, because—to us—completing a project on time and on budget was the normal business practice.

I didn't learn how *"not-normal"* and hard it was for others until I became a Sales Engineer and had to create network designs for IT departments I had never worked with. Selling hardware and software solutions to them was much harder than I imagined, because the majority didn't know how to create a successful design. They also didn't know the design was the heart of the project, which is why they had struggled and failed so much in the past.

The purpose of any computer network is to provide *"Services"* the employees of that company use, like File Sharing, Printing, and E-Mail. When you build or upgrade a network, you're either improving existing services, or introducing new ones the company needs. And there are only two reasons that justify spending the time, money, and other resources:

1. To solve a problem that the company is experiencing.
2. To deliver a new value that the company doesn't currently possess.

Number one is a *requirement*, and no project should ever be funded if it doesn't solve a problem, save money, or make money.

Number two is *desirable* if it can be done within the same budget. It's like a gift that the executives will love you for, because they weren't expecting it when they approved the project.

As a consultant, it was my job to teach our customers these concepts, so we could all work as one team to succeed. Too often, they would install new technologies on their own to *"see what happens,"* without a clear design for making those changes. That's like setting a goal without understanding how all the pieces work together, and you wouldn't handle a project in your home that way. If you wanted new lighting installed, you wouldn't start connecting fixtures and components without an understanding of how your house was wired.

Unfortunately, many IT departments don't understand how their networks are built, what will break them, or how to safely make changes without disrupting existing services. As a result, I had to ask probing questions to figure out those basics before I could design their project correctly.

Often, they were surprised or confused by how detailed a design needed to be, and I had to explain how important it was for creating success. Over time, I condensed the process into simple categories, because I saw that every successful project shared the same foundation:

1. A clear understanding of the accomplishment(s) the project needed to create.

2. Proven actions that work for that project, versus what people thought would work, heard from others, or worked the last time.

3. The understanding that research and facts were needed to overcome setbacks or failures, and that hoping, wishing, and wondering are not skills.

That foundational knowledge was what my customers were lacking, and why their projects in the past were finished late, didn't meet their expectations, or failed completely. That's also why they brought in consultants like me, who had the expertise they never learned on their own.

Projects And Goals Are The Same: After six months of consulting, I realized that what we called a project at work could also be called a goal for the company. Projects are designed to solve problems, and/or create new values, which was identical to what goals in our personal lives are supposed to do.

Nobody talked about goals that way, but—just like projects—they succeed or fail based on how we design them. So, I started thinking about how design skills for technology goals could be used as a system for achieving personal ones, and the concept of goal design was born.

Goal design uses a set of standards like project teams always have, so—whether you're making baby furniture, getting your Ph.D., or training for the Olympics—the method works for everyone.

This shift in mindset was a game-changer for my customers, because they were used to figuring out how to set and achieve a goal each time. This approach might sound overly simple, but once you have some practice, you start to recognize the power in it. Because of our experience in the past, we assume that goals and success must be more complex. For most of my life, Tribal Knowledge and Common Sense told me that was true, and I didn't know what to do about it.

But when we know what makes us feel successful (i.e., achieving great accomplishments) designing clear goals with Proven Actions is actually easy. And goal design gives us the ability to manage changes accurately, because we'll know how they affect our designs when we see them. That's how to quickly turn fear into facts to solve problems and keep progressing.

Gap Analysis and RDOM2: We don't have to reinvent how we plan for and design our goals each time, and the technique we're about to learn will show us a better way. I learned about Gap Analysis and RDOM2 from Project Management training and saw that they were more powerful when we use them together.

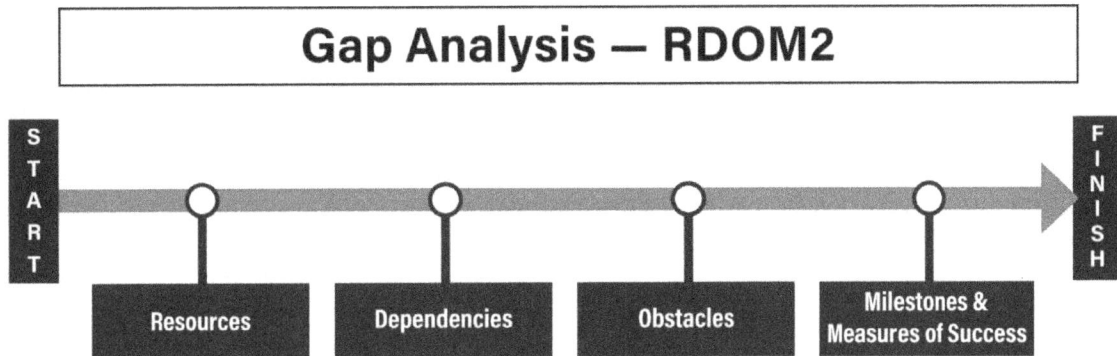

> ➤ **R**esources - People or things that help us.

> ➤ **D**ependencies - Resources we must use in a certain order to complete our goal.

> ➤ **O**bstacles – Resources or other things that keep us from starting or finishing a goal.

> ➤ **M**ilestones and **M**easures of Success - Standards that tell us we've completed a step in our goal, and a measurement to *prove* we did.

Gap Analysis is actually simple, because it's just a comparison between where we want to go, where we are right now, and the *Resources* we need to get there.

1. First, we define the Finish Line of our goal in detail, which is our Great Accomplishment.

2. Next we research, to find all the Proven Actions we need to achieve that.

3. Proven actions tell us the resources we need, like time, money, or *other resources*. Other resources are anything that isn't time or money, like tools, skills, or help from someone else.

4. Then we organize our complete list of resources into the RDOM2 categories in the middle, known as The Gap. That helps us do three things:

   ► Determine how and when we can get the resources we need.

   ► Clarify Proven Actions, to make sure they're the right ones and no others are missing. That's how to adjust our resource list as we go, to make sure it's always aligned to the actions we need to take.

   ► Find delays in our schedule, based on how and when we can get the resources we need to take our Proven Actions.

Some resources belong in more than one category, because they could be a *Dependency* and/or *Obstacle* at the same time. They could also change from one category to the other and knowing that gives us the agility to manage changes when they happen. Having this knowledge from the start enables us to schedule everything, take action as soon as possible, and see when our design needs updating.

A schedule for actions and a deadline for when to finish are critical so we don't take too much time to succeed with our goal. If we do, it could turn it into a *later* idea, and—as we've learned—*later* usually turns out to be *never*.

Too often people start figuring out these details after they've taken *unproven actions*, and then don't know how to recover. That's the goal ***setting*** technique we grew up using, and you can see how difficult and inefficient it is compared to the goal ***design*** technique with Gap Analysis and RDOM2.

For example, if you ask someone what their goal is, they might say "*lose 20 pounds.*" That sounds like a clear vision for a great accomplishment, but when you ask what their plan is, they say things like "*I don't know, eat less and go to the gym, I guess. We'll see what happens.*"

And they're right. We will see what happens when their lack of vision and design don't create the progress they're hoping, wishing, and wondering for. And this cycle repeats itself over and over, because we were trained as children to focus on the finish line instead of the specific actions needed to get there.

We need a better way to manage the details and the timeline of a goal, and most importantly fix any issues before they get in the way and put us on pause. Gap Analysis and RDOM2 solve those problems by creating a picture of what our design will do, or where it's lacking and needs more work.

I Need to Lose "Some Weight." If we had a goal to weigh 200 pounds, that would be a clear statement of the great accomplishment we wanted. That becomes the finish line of the Gap Analysis, and no one has to figure out or interpret what 200 pounds means.

But vague statements like "*I need to lose some weight*" don't give us a finish line that we can understand and plan for, just like "*a lot of money*" doesn't tell us how many dollars we're talking about. Since there's no definition for "*some weight,*" there are no specific actions we can take to get there, which means we can't create a design to guide us.

That's why it's so hard to achieve a goal that isn't specific, and how being unclear keeps us from managing changes or knowing the right actions to take when we try. And isn't that how we failed ourselves in the past, by not having a clear plan and quitting when we thought we'd done enough, gone far enough, or couldn't "*see ourselves*" doing any more?

So, once we clearly define the finish line we're planning for, the next step is to clearly define our starting point. In the case of weight loss, it's simple, and we only need a bathroom scale to do it. If the scale says 220 pounds today, we know our Gap Analysis will be designed for losing 20. With that clarity, we can start organizing our resources into the RDOM2 categories and making a plan to achieve our 20-pound weight loss.

Gap Analysis and RDOM2 remove all of the guessing about what we're really doing, what the pieces are we need to organize, and how to do it. We're not *"trying"* to lose *"some weight,"* we're creating a specific design to lose 20 pounds. By designing this way, it's easy to see what you're doing, what you should be doing, and when you need help to know what to do.

It's also easy to see if you've made any mistakes, left something out, and specifically when F.U.D. shows up and tries to put you on pause. The way to know all this is by asking *"how do I know,"* when you think you know what you're doing, or you get scared and think you're failing.

"How do I know this is the answer, or a problem" will keep you from getting stuck and not knowing how to continue.

Think of a goal design like a to-do list, a list of parts, a roadmap, and a schedule with a deadline. Then, gap analysis gives you an understanding that's much more powerful than a simple list of tasks, and that's how it creates the vision for success we haven't had before.

That vision empowers you to focus your energy on *how* to take Proven Actions, versus not being sure *what* they are or if they're the right ones.

Designing Weight Loss With Gap Analysis And RDOM2: Below are some specific RDOM2 components you might define in a weight loss goal, and an example of how to think through and design all the pieces. While you're reading, think about a goal you have now, had in the past, or are pausing on.

> ➤ How could you structure it like this one?

> ➤ What problems would it solve for you?

> ➤ What new value would it bring to you?

Now is the time to start practicing, so these tools and techniques start to become yours and feel like something you use to make changes in your life today.

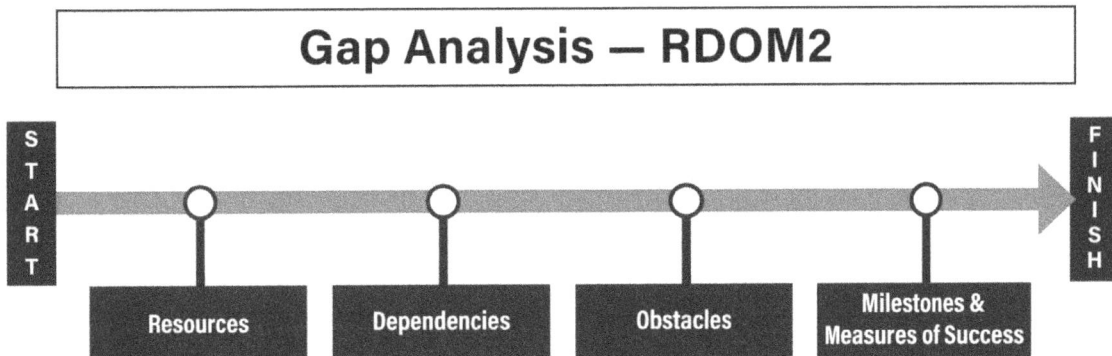

Gap Analysis — RDOM2

START — Resources — Dependencies — Obstacles — Milestones & Measures of Success — FINISH

Resources: Internet Access, Meal Plan, Family Support, Money.

Dependencies: Money, Gym Membership, and Personal Trainer

Obstacles: Nachos And Beer, Planning Meals For The Week, Family Support.

Milestones and Measures of Success: Losing 1.5 Pounds Per Week, as verified by the bathroom scale.

That's how easy it is to start standardizing your goals and changing your life. Each category may need to be more detailed than these, but you can see how quickly the picture of what you're doing comes into focus.

Resources: For this goal, we would need Internet access to research meal plans that work for us, plan our meals ahead of time to avoid eating the wrong things, and be supported by our family so we don't give up. We also need money to afford a membership at the gym, because we want to work with a personal trainer.

Dependencies: These are also *Resources*, but our ability to use them is dependent on having at least one other resource first. In this example, we want to work out at a gym with a personal trainer and doing that is *dependent* on having the money first.

If we don't have the money, it changes the actions we can take until we do, and we need to know that as quickly as possible. That helps us think about alternative *Resources* we can use, and whether that changes the schedule for when we can complete our goal.

For example, if we could start our exercise plan without the gym and trainer, while saving money to afford them later, that would be better than not exercising at all. And if we tried and failed to make progress on our own, that would tell us to do more research into the actions we could take until we can afford the gym and trainer.

Setbacks and failures should call us into action, and when we're mission focused, they will. We won't feel the urge to stop or give up, because we know there are other paths we can find and take. There are many fitness and diet coaches on the Internet, which is a free *Resource* that we have access to. Because waiting is not a skill, we have to keep researching actions to make sure we're not pausing without a plan.

Dependencies don't tell us to give up, they only create perspective on what we need, where the weak parts of our goals are, and what we need to research to get the facts.

When you organize your designs by thinking that way, it's much easier to see and plan for *Dependencies* from the beginning. That way they don't become *Obstacles* that affect what you do or if you give up and stop. We can't let our designs become abstract thoughts that get shut down by the caveperson, so we need to identify and organize *Dependencies* as soon as possible.

Since *Dependencies* are controlled by having other *Resources* first, like money, they show us how to schedule our goals. If we can't afford the gym and trainer now, but we know we can save enough money in six months, we know how to design our schedule. Then we focus on the actions we can take now, like exercising at home using free training from the Internet. You might even find that the gym and trainer are not needed, which is a great example of being agile with a Changemaker mindset.

Once we have the money, and still want to work at the gym with a trainer, we can change our schedule to include that. With that level of understanding and control there will be very little confusion or delay in our goal designs.

Another thing we need to understand, while waiting on a *Dependency,* is if there can be a setback or failure by not taking an action that is time sensitive. If the gym is having a sale that expires in a week, we would want to know that so we could prove whether it affects us. If we could save 35% on gym fees it would be worth using a credit card to pay for them now. We might pay $50 in interest charges on our credit card to do that, but if we saved $300 on gym and trainer fees, we would actually be $250 ahead for the year.

But of course, you have to pay that credit card debt off to make your credit work for you as a *Resource.*

Using the credit card accomplishes two things we wouldn't have had by waiting and not buying during the sale:

1. We start our goal with the gym and trainer we want to work with now.

2. We save $250 to use as a new *Resource* for other goals later.

Knowing all these things gives us a power and control that's huge, because it eliminates most of the unknown, unclear, and abstract thoughts we've always struggled with. When changes happen that we can't predict, we'll know how they affect our design and be able to deal with them more easily.

Changes can affect the *Resources* we have, need, or turn existing ones into a *Dependency* or *Obstacle.* But when we create a goal design, we're like an Architect, and can easily redesign things to keep them progressing toward success.

All our behaviors of the past got us to where we are today, and the purpose of a goal design with Gap Analysis and RDOM2 is to make sure we don't find ourselves repeating those behaviors.

Obstacles: When you hear that word, you might think of a big thing that stands between you and where you want to go. Because we think they're not movable or changeable, we might believe that *Obstacles* mean our goal can't be achieved. We see them as abstract and unclear, instead of a signal to do research and define them to get the facts. Once again, the caveperson shuts us down quickly to save brain fuel, and we either choose less-great things to work for or give up on choosing at all.

We have to view *Obstacles* differently and start thinking of them as research opportunities. We need to understand how to work around or eliminate them, because *Obstacles* affect us in two ways:

1. They keep us from *starting* goals.

2. They keep us from *finishing* goals.

Knowing that at the start of our design process gives us power, because once we know how they could affect us we can make alternative choices. For weight loss, we need to plan our meals ahead of time to keep from eating the things that made us need this goal in the first place. Continuing to eat the old foods would be an *Obstacle* that keeps us from *starting* our goal, because what we eat is the most important part of controlling our weight.

When I weighed 285 pounds, my diet was the biggest *Obstacle* I had to learn about. I didn't know that what I ate was the cause of the problem, and my ignorance was how I got to be so fat to begin with. Because it happened over a long period of time, I didn't see it coming, and without knowing about food as an *Obstacle* I was never doing the right things to start my goal.

I told myself and others I was dieting and went to the gym like we had always heard we should, without Proving what those words meant. I spent a lot of time trying to burn calories at the gym while continuing to eat the wrong foods and take in too many calories.

I finally learned that if you don't eat the calories in the first place, you don't have to work them off. It's easier to not eat them than to use your time and energy *Resources* to remove what should have never been there in the first place. That sounds so obvious now, but *everything* does when you have the facts on your side.

The other challenge with *Obstacles* is how they keep us from *finishing* a goal.

Back to our weight-loss example, if we ate all the right foods six days a week but continued having nachos and beer on our bowling nights, we would sabotage the positive changes we made. We couldn't *finish* our weight loss goal because unneeded snacks would be an *Obstacle* between us and the finish line.

Worse than that, one bad habit eventually leads us to others, and we could easily give up on our goals that way. With food it's easy for one *"cheat night"* to become our normal behavior again, and the emotional letdown from that makes us feel like our hard work isn't *"working."* That's how we get disappointed and depressed with goals, when we don't have a design that shows us the big picture, and where an *Obstacle* might exist.

When we don't know what our *Obstacles* are, or that we can deal with them, we can't see how to get started or finished like we thought we could. We feel like we've done all the things we can *"think of,"* but *"**It's** not working."*

That's when our plans become unclear and abstract and turn into *long-term* ideas we push off until *later*. After a few of those experiences we start to think *"we're not good enough"* and settle into a life of smaller accomplishments. Once again, that's called *Rationalization*.

That's why we are the first Obstacle we need to be aware of, because we've been practicing being on pause instead of researching to design the answers we need. Keep in mind there is no *"**It**,"* only you, your goal designs, and Proven Actions. Success is created *through you*, and it starts with designing detailed goals you're in control of.

Understanding that *Obstacles* exist and how they work actually gives us power. And we need that, because our *Resources, Dependencies,* and *Milestones and Measures* can't compensate for what *Obstacles* can do to us. Understanding that is the difference between a setback you can *"see yourself"* recovering from, and a failed goal you give up on *forever*.

Milestones and Measures of Success: These are the M2 part of the RDOM2 system, and they're how we prove we're making the progress we should be. They show us when we've accomplished a step in our design, using a proven measuring tool we trust.

If we expect to lose 1.5 pounds per week, that would be called our *Milestone*. It's like a marker in a race, that tells you how far you've gone on the course. The *Measure of Success* would be checking our weight on the bathroom scale, to prove that we've hit the *Milestone*.

Thinking we feel lighter, without using a measuring tool, takes us back to hoping, wishing, and wondering about progress. But with proven measures, if we don't see the losses we're expecting to see, we know immediately to double-check our actions. In the case of weight loss, we might be eating more calories than we realize, if we're not measuring portions, and the measure of success will tell us when that might be happening.

Another *Resource* in our goal would be knowing that weight loss is often not consistent and could take longer than we expect. We may not see a 1.5-pound loss each week, but a four or five-pound loss by the end of week three. The bathroom scale is our primary measuring tool but understanding how our body reacts to dieting is the most important thing to know for this type of goal.

It may take a month to see consistent losses on the scale, so we should understand if there are other *Measurements* we can use, like how our clothes fit.

Often times, the scale won't change on a regular schedule, but our pants will fit better. Each person's body can work differently for weight loss, and we would need to figure out how ours works to plan accurately and not feel defeated. That's an example of a continual goal design process, to be aware of and ready for changes when they're needed.

This is a simple example of how to design and manage a goal using Gap Analysis and RDOM2, but you can see how easy it becomes to add more detail once you break it down into organized sections.

And the technique gets easier by continually asking these:

1. What other *Actions* does this design need?

2. What other *Resources* do I need?

3. What other *Dependencies* exist?

4. What other *Obstacles* are there, and ***what could become one***?

All *Obstacles* won't be obvious until you think about what keeps you from starting or finishing your goal. And a *Resource* or *Dependency* could become an *Obstacle* along the way, which is something else to think about in your design. As an example, if your trainer moves away and the gym doesn't have another available, that could become an *Obstacle* that keeps you from finishing your goal.

But if you realized the knowledge you gained from working with a trainer had made you your own *Resource,* you could exercise on your own without having to stop. At worst, you could modify your schedule to extend the deadline of the goal, and still call it a success when you finished. Things will change without warning or permission, and we have to be able to change with them to keep our goals progressing toward success.

Gap Analysis and RDOM2 validate the old saying that "*practice makes perfect,*" but takes it a step further to say, "*perfect practice makes perfect.*" And that means perfect for what you and your goals need, not some idea of what others say is perfection. The way to create perfect practice is by not being afraid to make mistakes, and to have a continual design mentality to find the solutions your goal needs.

Goal Design Is Like A Party: Creating a successful goal design is as easy as creating and changing your list for a party. That list is a goal design, and if you've ever made one to buy food and other items for a party, you've successfully managed a Gap Analysis using RDOM2.

➤ You visualized the Finish Line, which were all the items you needed for the party, and all the people you needed to help you.

➤ You compared those to your Starting Point, which were the people and things already available to you.

➤ You made your list based on the gap between what you needed, and what you had.

In other words:

You've already succeeded with everything in this chapter.

You designed all the *Resources, Dependencies, Obstacles* and *Milestones and Measures of Success* needed to make that party succeed, without knowing how powerful you were.

Designing a goal is just like organizing a party, and the more you think about the things we've discussed the easier and more obvious it will become for you. And there's one more benefit that we didn't cover. The more skilled you become with Gap Analysis and RDOM2, the more ***time*** you save by being efficient with planning, designing, and taking actions.

Managing our time, money, and other resources affects our levels of success, which is another lesson we weren't taught as kids. That's why things felt so unclear in the past, so we'll talk about how goal setting gets more organized and accelerated by better *Resource* management in Chapter 9: Creating a Budget for Success.

You won't realize how much time and effort you've wasted until you practice being efficient and purposeful now. Once that happens, you won't be able to live the old way, and knowing how and when to do the right things will start to feel like successes by themselves.

Creating a Budget for Success

When we go on vacation, most of us have to follow a budget. In fact, we have at least two and sometimes three types of budgets we need to work with. The first is how much *money* we can spend, which might sound like all we need to think about. But it's not, because the *time* we have off from work, the travel time to and from our vacation spot, and the activities we need time to do there are equally important. Then, if we're travelling with others who have different financial or time constraints than we do, we have to take those factors into account as well.

Our time, money, and other resources—like our friend's budgets—are all dependent on each other. Therefore, the way we plan for and use them determines the amount of fun or frustration we will have. To make our vacation the best it can be, we need to research the facts, prove that they have the value we need, and be prepared to make changes along the way.

That sounds a lot like goal design, because that's exactly what it is. A vacation is a set of goals we design to fit together, using a budget of time, money, and other resources.

In Economics, the Principle of Scarcity states that we have an unlimited desire for goods and services, but limited resources to create them. To maximize the value our resources bring, we have to use them in the most efficient way and keep looking for ways to improve that.

In this chapter, we'll see that all goals *must* have a budget to maximize the successes we want, because we'll always have limited resources. Even when we become excellent at building and maintaining our *Three Pillars of Success,* we can still be held back by how we use our Budget for Success.

We Can't Afford to Waste Time: Think about what happens when we waste our time. Not only can we never get it back, but we limit the number of great accomplishments we can create.

Imagine we design a goal on January 1st that will take all year to complete, but then put ourselves on pause until April 1st. What is the result of that choice, and how long does it affect us? The 90 days we waste is the time we should be making progress, and that part of the work still needs to be done. But by wasting our time, we're left doing 12 months of work in 9, or more likely pushing out our completion date from December 31st of this year to April 1st of next. Wasting time means we can't do as many goals in the same period of time, because we still have to accomplish all the things we should have done when we were pausing.

But that's not the real problem.

Imagine we can only afford to do that one goal this year, because it requires all our free time. That means we can't start another until April 2nd of next year, because we put ourselves behind schedule *this* year. That one 90-day pause we took could affect our progress for years, if all our goals take a year to complete. Then the question becomes "*what did we lose out on achieving by creating a delay that shouldn't have existed?*"

Can we work harder to get caught up and stop that cycle of delays? If not, for how many more years will we be behind on achieving goals, and will that create feelings of frustration and failure that put us on pause without a plan again?

This happens to college students all the time. When they take fewer classes per semester, take semesters off, or can't get into classes because they're full, it extends their four-year degree program into five or six years. That's an inefficient use of their time, and it delays them from taking the next steps toward a career or graduate program. Graduating later than expected could also cause them to miss opportunities for great accomplishments they may never even know about.

We can't predict the future, so you might think that worrying about missing something you don't even know about is also inefficient. I would have to agree, however, what I'm stressing here is that our time is invaluable, irreplaceable, and it affects our future successes. To create the most success we can, on the schedule we want, we can't treat our time like there are no *penalties* for wasting it.

The decisions we make today limit the choices we can make tomorrow, next month, or next year in some cases. Wasting time can create a chain reaction of events some call the Domino Effect. That means a certain choice now can cause an outcome that forces us to make a choice in the future we normally wouldn't, may not want, or can't avoid. When one domino falls, it makes others fall with it, and the questions we must answer are these:

1. Will our choices today create, delay, or deflate our great accomplishments?

2. How do we know?

> ➤ If we buy an expensive car, we can't spend as much on our rent or mortgage until the car is paid off, or until we make more money.

> ➤ If we go on vacation, we can't pay off our student loans until we earn more money to make up for what we shouldn't have spent.

Buying cars and going on vacations can force us to make choices in the future that could have been easily avoided. And if we don't think about the outcomes they'll create over the next 3, 5, or 10 years, we could limit our ability to succeed in ways we never imagined.

That's not worrying about a future we can't predict; it's how we need to think and design our choices to *protect that future.*

The Elimination Effect: Under normal circumstances, I would have graduated from college in May of 1990. I would have earned a Business Management degree and begun a long and steady rise through the corporate world by September of that year. I'm confident in saying that because I grew up near Washington D.C., and back then there was no shortage of jobs for new business graduates.

But I wasn't like my peers, and always hated school, so instead of celebrating that May I was working two jobs and struggling financially. By June of '91, I had run out of ideas and money. I had no career skills, no idea of who or what I was, and no plan for how to fix all that.

My best friend from high school had become an Electrical Engineer by then and was recruited by the Navy for their nuclear power program. Through him, I learned that the Navy offered technical jobs for people without college degrees, and the G.I. Bill program to earn money for college. I decided the five years I had wasted were enough, and I needed an immediate change.

By March of '93 I was stationed on a warship in Long Beach California and wondering what I had done to my life. Military service wasn't what I hoped for, and my job as an Electronics Technician wasn't as great as our instructors in school said it would be.

That's when I learned about the Elimination Effect. Similar to the Domino Effect, this one goes a step further to a place you may never have thought of. Instead of a choice now causing us to make others in the future, the Elimination Effect shows us the basket of choices *we've eliminated from our lives* by making the wrong choices to begin with.

> ➤ By not graduating from college with my peers, I didn't have the education to use in the early days of the Internet and Dot.Com fields. They were exploding with opportunities then, and I missed out on every one of them by being in the Navy where I wasn't free to pursue them.

> ➤ By not graduating from college with my peers, I also couldn't serve as an officer in the Navy. I didn't receive training in how to be a manager and leader, because as an enlisted person I was *eliminated* from that path. Learning management and leadership skills on my own was harder and took longer, because I didn't start with the same foundation as young officers did.

➤ And by not graduating from college with my peers, and building my career sooner, I was late in saving money for a house. My Personal Identity wasn't strong enough to support me in *"adult"* thinking and acting back then, and I was 35 years old by the time I thought about buying one. By waiting so long I ***eliminated*** my ability to buy the kind I wanted and had to settle for one I didn't like or want. Prices had grown beyond what I could afford by then, and there was nothing I could do to change that reality.

With ***one decision*** to not complete my education, I eliminated my ability to create the best version of all the important choices people make in life: Career, Home, and Retirement. And those mistakes can never be undone, because those moments have passed and can't be recreated.

Think about that in the context of *"everything happens for a reason"* from Chapter 7. We either make proven choices that create the results we want, or we're left with choices that are less desirable, and which affect our successes in ways we can't control.

Our time is the most valuable resource we have because of the Domino and Elimination Effects. That's why there's no time to waste when it comes to creating success. Now I'm not suggesting that we should speed up the pace of our lives, but that we can't afford to do things that don't lead us to great accomplishments.

As an example, you would never work 40 hours at a job if they only paid you for 20. Why, then, would you spend twice the time to get a goal done when the delay doesn't improve the outcome and it's *within your control* to do it on time?

It's true we can take time off and pause when we're in control of our time, but we can't spend it randomly or carelessly now that we know how that affects what we can do in the future.

One Life to Give: When we waste our time, we limit the speed at which we can achieve our goals over the course of our lifetime. Since success is about achieving great accomplishments at our highest levels, we simply can't afford to waste our time ***at any time***.

Otherwise, it's easy to put ourselves on pause and start thinking (rationalizing) about less, doing less, and accepting less from ourselves.

Now that we see how choice making affects us with regard to time, we need to think about and design our choices from a lifetime perspective. As I said earlier, we need to understand the effects our choices will bring in 3, 5, or 10 years, and of course prove those choices like everything else we've talked about. Since we only have one life to give to our goals, we need to create that life in a way that gets us all the results we want. In computer networking we call that *Deterministic Design*, which means we determine the specific outcomes we want, and work backward to build everything to support those.

If you're 22 years, old and just starting a job, how accomplished and successful could you be by age 32 if you thought this way? Imagine if you used every month of those 10 years to improve your skills in a deterministic way, so they built upon each other? How much better would your life be than your peers, who were waiting to be told what to do and when?

Now change those numbers to 32 and 42, or 42 and 52. No matter your age you can still create calculated outcomes by designing the right changes for yourself without waiting. And I know 10 years is a long and abstract time to think about, so to get through this without the caveperson shutting us down, let's break it down.

Week, Month, Quarter, And Year: If you know how colleges work, you already know how to use this technique. To get through four years of school, you break it into four year-long pieces, and treat each one as a goal that qualifies you for the next. Each year has up to 3 semesters, or four quarters, and you plan the number of classes to take in each segment so you can finish by the end of the year.

That's the same process you can use now for organizing your time and actions to achieve great accomplishments. When you break a goal down into periods of time that are easier to think about, like a week, month, or quarter, it becomes easier to plan for what you can get done in a year. And that skill helps you think about and organize goals that add up to choices for 3, 5, or 10 years from now. It doesn't feel or work any differently, because the skill is to manage plans, actions and changes over time, regardless of how long that is.

Whatever needs to be done in a year can be divided into four quarters. Each quarter divides into three months, and they're made up of four weeks. Looking at the year that way lets you easily make a schedule for developing skills and getting the work done in the same way you would as a college student. And like a student, if you miss a deadline, you'll know immediately how it affects the rest of the month, quarter, or year.

That big-picture vision guides you in either working harder to finish the year on time or prepares you for being late and not finishing until next year. Either way, you'll always know what's going on in your life, and most importantly why. Imagine the stress that takes away.

It's true we can't plan for everything that might happen in the future, but this technique is about planning for what we *do* know about, and what we *can* control now. That gives us a solid foundation for when unexpected changes show up, so we'll be better qualified to deal with them. It's hard for one element of a plan to ruin everything when we have the goal design skills to manage choices and changes.

That's why it's so important to treat our time as invaluable, irreplaceable, and our most powerful resource. I never thought that way growing up, because nobody ever talked about it like that. As kids, our time felt never-ending, and we only made decisions after someone or something prompted us. Instead of designing specific outcomes we wanted, and getting the skills to take Proven Actions, we reacted to the world around us and hoped, wished, and wondered about the future.

That's how the Domino and Elimination Effects came into our lives, and how over time we accepted them as normal outcomes. But that's *abnormal* when you understand the penalties created by thinking and acting that way. Since wasting time can't lead us to great accomplishments, we have to be aware of when we're doing it so we can stop.

When we're dedicated to learning new skills, and developing them at our highest levels, we'll become very accomplished and well-paid compared to others who aren't spending their time the same way. And when we look at windows of time like 3, 5, and 10 years, we'll know how to break them down into manageable pieces.

So, as we go forward in the chapter, ask yourself where you can start using your time in a better way, and the benefits you'll receive when you do. That's the power and control you get when you design your goals with a Budget for Success.

We Can't Afford to Waste Money: Now we need to talk about how money works as a resource in our Budget for Success, and how it's so closely connected to how we spend our time. I know it's obvious that if we waste money now, we don't have it to spend later, but the penalty for doing that is actually bigger than you think.

Like time, the way money works for us is affected by the Domino and Elimination Effects. We have to think about how we use our money, and the results we can create with it longer term like the 3, 5, and 10-year windows we talked about with time. By practicing being efficient with our time, it will be easier to remember to do it with our money.

Even billionaires think like this, which is how they got to be wealthy in the first place. They can't maintain their financial success by being on pause and "*seeing what happens*," so why would we continue doing that in our lives?

I was on pause without a plan for a long time and wasted a lot of money because I didn't understand the Domino and Elimination Effects. When you don't know things like that exist you don't spend time looking for them, which means you don't see their cause and effect relationships. When that's where your thoughts are, change can never happen because you don't have a clue you need it.

For a long time, I tried to buy feelings of accomplishment, without understanding that I was eliminating choices from my future. When we waste money like that, on things that don't get us closer to our great accomplishments, we still have to do the work that will. But by spending the money on the wrong things, we have to wait until *later* when we can make more money to do the right things.

We have to commit *time* in the future to earn that wasted money back, instead of spending the money in the future as a *Resource* for goals we would normally do then.

It's a ***double penalty***, because we're wasting time and money now, and also in the future, to get closer to one great accomplishment. And that's presuming we don't make other mistakes that keep us from making progress on the goal we delayed, by wasting the money to start with.

If that sounds confusing, let me sum it up: Wasting time or money at any time makes dominoes fall and eliminates choices that we may never be able to recover from. Even with plenty of money in the bank, wasting any of it limits the goals we can accomplish in the course of our lifetime. That means limiting the levels of success we can achieve, or the speed at which we can reach them.

No matter how much money we ever have, waste will never create more success in our lives.

We Can't Afford to Waste Other Resources: The concept of *Other Resources* simply means things that aren't time or money. Examples are skills, help from other people, or tools we need for our goal. And just like time and money, we have to plan for and treat *Other Resources* with the same respect for their value.

Imagine that I ask for your help to get part of my goal completed but can't commit to a time we can meet. If I keep rescheduling, and cancel on the days we planned for, how long will you tolerate that before taking back your offer to help? Your time is valuable, and I have to treat it that way if I expect you to share it with me.

When we need *Other Resources,* we have to think of them in terms of *Time, Tools*, and *Tolerance*.

➤ Are we respecting people's *time*?

➤ Are we respecting the *tools* they're lending us? Those could be physical, like a set of wrenches, or their knowledge about a problem we need to solve.

➤ Are we respecting their *tolerance*? As I said earlier, if I ask for your help, but don't respect your time, I'm going to lose your desire to help me.

Also, if we ask for someone's advice, or to teach us something, but then ignore what they say, we're not respecting them as a resource. They may not want to help us again if we keep doing that, so we need to make sure they're the proven resource we need before asking for their help.

No matter what the *Other Resource* is, if it's needed in our goal design, we have to treat it with respect. Wasting any *Resource* doesn't create greater successes, but using them efficiently does, which is the purpose of having a Budget for Success.

Qualifying Questions for Resources: In Chapter 3, we talked about qualifying our resources, and the three questions we need to do it:

1. Does this information/person/tool help me?

2. In what way does it help me?

3. For how long will it help me?

Using a Budget for Success to maximize our goal designs is when the value of qualifying our resources becomes much clearer. It might seem obvious to say that someone or something is a resource to us, but we need to prove that with specific details to make sure it's our best choice.

So, when you ask yourself, "*how much does this help me*," think of it as a two-part question:

➤ What *Problem* does this *Resource* solve for me?

➤ What new *Value* could this *Resource* create for me?

It's not enough to answer question 2 by saying "*a lot*" or "*in all the ways I need,*" because that's not detailed enough to tell us the full story. Instead, you have to tell yourself the problem it solves, and any new value it creates.

An example from our weight loss goal in Chapter 8 was our credit card to pay for gym fees. By doing that during the sale we saved $250 for the year, even though we paid $50 in interest charges. The credit card as a *Resource* helped us solve the problem of getting a gym membership and trainer now and created a new value by saving money we can use on other goals later.

Asking ourselves about problem solving, and new value creation, is another skill to learn for our budgeting. Not every resource will create something new we didn't expect, but each one ***must solve a problem for us*** at the level we need.

If it can't do that, we have to look for a better resource that can, because our goal design can't be effective without it.

When we design a goal, we have to think about all our *Resources* as *limited*, so we don't misuse them to create delays we could avoid. Most importantly, we don't want to eliminate choices from our future by not understanding what we're doing or what it leads to later in our lives.

Creating greater successes, at faster speeds, involves everything we've talked about in the chapters so far. In the end, though, we will always be limited the most by how we plan for and use our Budget for Success.

CHAPTER 10

Building Your Three Pillars for Success

Congratulations! You've come a long way and learned a lot of new ideas. Now it's time to put them all together, so you can start making these changes in your life today.

Step 1: Define your Great Accomplishment

Example: "I want to finish the Marine Corps Marathon (MCM) in Washington D.C."

That was a great accomplishment my wife created for herself, and it took her four years to achieve. She had run 5k and 10-mile races before then and decided that a full marathon was her next-level accomplishment. Having served as a Marine in the first Gulf War made completing the MCM particularly meaningful to her, and her only question was how to get it done.

That's the key when you define great accomplishments. They must be meaningful to be considered great, and when they are you're motivated to find the proven actions needed to complete them. When they feel like something you can't live without, they motivate you to perform at your highest levels. Once you find something that important, you'll automatically want to get organized and start completing it.

When our goals are designed like that, they don't even feel like work. So, if you find yourself feeling unmotivated, or overwhelmed by one, that's a *signal* for change. You need to stop and ask yourself what makes that great accomplishment so great. If you can't answer clearly and passionately, you're probably on the wrong track. That's okay, because it's better to regroup than to waste effort and resources on a goal that isn't meaningful to you.

To find what matters to you most, in each area of your life, you have to make time to think about it. Identifying great accomplishments is a skill that requires practice, and it might take some time for you to learn it. That's normal, so don't think you have to do this quickly. The most important part of creating real success is developing the skill to identify what is most important to you.

Without that practice you'll make the wrong choices and find yourself on pause without a plan. It's also a signal that F.U.D. is keeping you from finding the answers, so ignore it, and keep thinking about what your great accomplishments are.

Step 2: Personal Identity – Identify the Type of Person who can achieve the great accomplishment you want and become that type.

- What skills do they have?
- What level are those skills at?
- How do I develop them?

Example: "I want to be a Marathon Runner"

My wife is not a natural runner. She has to train for races to build her stamina each time, and that was especially true for the Marine Corps Marathon (MCM). She was passionate about finishing it, but also not sure about three important things:

1. Could she run 26.2 miles?
2. What was the average per-mile pace she could maintain?
3. Would that be enough to "*Beat the Bridge*?"

Like all of us, she wondered if she could become the *Type of Person* she needed to be.

When marathons are held in cities, they close the streets to traffic to create the course. But there's a limit to how long they can do that, and in the case of the MCM it's seven hours. However, there's a bigger challenge to overcome.

It's called "*Beating the Bridge*," which refers to reaching the 14th Street Bridge in Washington D.C. before the police have to re-open the streets. The bridge is 20 miles into the race, and you only have 5 hours to get there. That means maintaining (or beating) a 14 minute-per-mile pace for 80% of the race. If you can't do that, race volunteers pick you up in a van and remove you from the course.

Beating the bridge isn't a problem for experienced marathoners, but for first timers it's not just a physical barrier, but a mental one. My wife was determined to overcome both of those challenges, so she changed her P.I. and skills training to become the type of person who could do it.

But it took four years for her to be ready for race day. Building her skills took time, consistent effort, and recovery from injury. She needed help from coaches in a training program, and then had to dedicate herself to doing the work. It wasn't easy, and it didn't happen fast, but she earned that great accomplishment by never giving up.

That's the key for achieving goals in *any* area of our lives. Changing our P.I. to overcome challenges, and working to get the skills we need, is the only way it works. Unfortunately, we want changes to happen quickly, and we get impatient when they don't. When change doesn't happen fast enough, we get discouraged, embarrassed, and overwhelmed. We start thinking that maybe we're not "***good enough***" to achieve that type of success, and we sometimes give up.

The good news is that only happens when we don't know how to change our P.I. to become the type of person we want to be.

To stop those negative feelings, we have to ask ourselves these questions:

1. How do I *know* this won't work?

2. How do I *know* it won't work this time?

3. What are the *proven methods* that will work for me?

It took my wife four years to complete the MCM, because she couldn't run 26.2 miles the first year she tried. In year two, she broke her ankle and couldn't continue training. She joined a marathon training group in year three, to get the coaching she realized she needed, but still couldn't go more than 12 miles. That didn't stop her, though, because finishing that race was so important. Her plan was to keep working until she succeeded, because she knew there was a way to get it done.

In year four she tried a different training group and was finally able to finish the 20-mile practice runs. She completed the MCM in 2013 and proved to herself she could become a Marathoner.

Ooh Rah, Theresa. Semper Fi.

That's how P.I. works for all of us, and for any great accomplishment:

1. Identify the *Type of Person* who can achieve the great accomplishment you want.

2. Understand the *Skills* they have that you need.

3. Develop those skills, or upgrade the ones you have, *to the Levels They Need to Be.*

4. Get help from *Qualified Resources* that have done what you want to do.

5. Always *Find the Facts*, and never give in to the feelings of F.U.D.

Step 1: Great Accomplishment

Step 2: Personal Identity

Step 3: Identify the Fears, Uncertainties, and Doubts that will keep you from changing.

When we make changes to our P.I., F.U.D. will automatically get in our way. It's that *Safety Mechanism* we can't turn off, so we need to recognize when it's happening. We have to see it as a *signal* to take action and get the facts to make the right decisions.

Keep in mind what our *Cycle of Limits* does, when we're not paying attention.

The cycle works backward from Pillar to 3 to 1:

- It starts with our fears, uncertainties, and doubts, which we call F.U.D., telling us to avoid the things we fear and don't understand.

- F.U.D. then influences our Personal Identity (P.I.), which is Pillar 2. P.I. tells us the *type of person* we are, and the *kinds of goals* we can accomplish. F.U.D. says each type of person can only do certain things, which is how we hit mental boundaries that limit what we think we can achieve.

- Limited goals mean we create limited successes. That reinforces our belief in the wrong Recipe for Success, which says it's defined by having "*a lot of money*" that we aren't good enough to earn.

When we believe our goals are limited by who we are, it reinforces the belief that we can't create a better life than the one we have now. To turn that downward spiral into a *Cycle of Success*, we have to start with the Facts.

Remember my roller coaster experience with the Loch Ness Monster? I was sure I would die if I rode it, even though no one got hurt for the 20 minutes I stood there watching. But even my firsthand evidence wasn't powerful enough to override what F.U.D. was telling me. Only the strength of Peer Pressure got me to go later in the day. That really meant I had F.U.D. about being teased for the rest of the school year, not that I overcame my fear of the ride on my own.

You might argue that at the age of 12 I wasn't expected to have the skills to overcome my F.U.D., and I would agree. However, it wasn't my age that was the issue. It's because our instinct tells us to avoid things we don't understand, in favor of the ones we do. "*Better Safe than Sorry*" is the belief that has guided us since we were kids, while feeling like our normal decision-making process. Our friends and families reinforced that message, and with the help of our caveperson brain, we let it become our reality.

At the age of 12, I could have made better choices if I had been trained to. Because I wasn't, I struggled with F.U.D. most of my life and it affected my ability to create success. Think about that for a moment. How many great accomplishments have you walked away from because you weren't sure of something and didn't get the facts to figure it out?

There's no way to know for sure, but one thing is clear: We have no time to waste when it comes to creating a successful life, and our fears, uncertainties, and doubts will never help us do that.

Instead, we have to practice the skills for researching and finding the facts about things that make us fearful, unsure, and doubtful. That's how to turn them into facts, understanding, and direction for creating greater success.

➢ **F**ear becomes **F**acts.

➢ **U**ncertainty becomes **U**nderstanding.

➢ **D**oubt becomes **D**irection.

Step 1: Great Accomplishments

Step 2: Personal Identity

Step 3: Turn F.U.D. into Facts

Step 4: Turn Great Accomplishments into *Now* ideas.

In Chapter 6, we talked about how the caveperson inside us limits the brain fuel we can use to solve problems. That's designed to keep us safe, not successful, and we need that fuel to create great accomplishments. We also need it to change our P.I. and skills, and to find the facts to overcome our F.U.D.

We need more brain fuel to turn our ideas into actions we can take ***Now***.

Once we've done that, we have to keep our momentum going so we don't *Get Put on Pause Without A Plan*. We need the facts about everything we're doing, so that new ideas don't become ***abstract*** or feel ***unsafe***. When we're not sure about ourselves, or our great accomplishments, ideas can easily get pushed away until "***Later***." That's not a date on the calendar we can plan for, but it is how we classify things when F.U.D. is controlling us.

The easiest way to fight back is by following this rule: When an idea is unclear, or you're not sure what to do with it, it's a *signal* to do research and get the facts.

Feeling unclear means your caveperson is stopping you from thinking, and we've paused like that for so long it feels like our normal decision-making process. It is normal, but it's also the one that leads us to mediocre lives we don't know how to change. "*Normal*" leads us nowhere and makes us think this is the best we can do for ourselves.

And then there are *Labels*. Terms like *Short-term*, *Long-term*, *Dream*, and *Ultimate Goal* don't help us succeed more or faster. But when we're unsure of ourselves they make us feel like we're "*doing something*." Really, we're just thinking about less, doing less, and accepting lower standards for our lives. Labels don't make our goals, or us, work any better, so we can't fall into the trap of thinking that they do.

When you get stuck trying to think your way through a problem, it might be the signal that you need help. A coach or mentor, that has done what you want to do, is the quickest way to succeed. Don't wait to get one, because qualified help is the most efficient way to build the skills you need for changing your P.I.

Don't push unfamiliar or unclear ideas away. Push through them to find the facts, and the proven actions for your goal designs that you can take ***Now***.

Step 1: Great Accomplishments

Step 2: Personal Identity

Step 3: Turn F.U.D. into Facts

Step 4: Turn Great Accomplishments into *Now* ideas.

Step 5: Change what you say to determine where you go

In Chapter 7, we talked about how what you say determines where you go, and how the way we talk to ourselves either *creates* or *deflates* our great accomplishments.

Language is the most powerful tool we have, and many of us were never taught to use it the right way. We have to listen to what we say, to ourselves and about ourselves, so we don't damage our ability to build skills for success.

Qualifiers are the biggest problem we need to listen for and stop using. They're the words that dilute the meaning of **action statements** and deflate our ability to create great accomplishments. I say deflate because we can't design goals to achieve great accomplishments by using insecure language that makes us think about less, do less, and accept less. You can't get a little bit pregnant, but we keep using qualifiers as though you can become a little bit successful.

Examples of qualifiers are:

- I'm **kinda** doing my own business.

- I'm **sorta like** an Entrepreneur.

- I'm **trying** to change some things.

Kinda, sorta like, and *trying* aren't direct and purposeful words, and if you think about the people you call successful, they didn't get where they are using language like that. Qualifiers soften our message in a way that says we aren't committed because we don't feel in control. That's the sign of a P.I. boundary that tells us that we're not good enough to go further, and we should stay right where we are.

"*Just*" is another qualifier we need to listen for and stop using. When we use it, what we're doing is asking for relief. We're frustrated or scared by our circumstances, and we don't feel any control.

➤ *I just want a break*

➤ *I just want to go home.*

➤ *I just wish life wasn't so hard.*

Like all qualifiers, "*Just*" is a sign that F.U.D. is telling us to think about less, do less, and accept less. That's our signal to figure out what our fear is so we can find the facts and become empowered. Again, it's always the caveperson and F.U.D. giving us a path back to safety, so we have to fight against those feelings by researching the facts.

Remember that Ray Kroc, founder of McDonalds, started his career over at the age of 52. And he did it at a time when it was hard to start a franchise. That didn't stop him, though, and he worked diligently for seven years to be able to buy out his partners and become the sole owner of the company.

When I wanted to go to Crossfit I thought it was "**too soon**," because I was so fat. I was sure I had to lose weight first, to be able to work out and lose weight. I told myself I needed time to "***get in shape***," before I could go to the gym to get in shape. It sounds crazy when you read it like this, but those are the kinds of feelings we get when our caveperson and F.U.D. cause us to be afraid. We literally talk ourselves out of success, and into the arms of safety without knowing it.

Remember How Failure Talk Sounds: You don't have to choose between having money, happiness, success, or anything else. You can have all the things you want in life by ***designing them to coexist***, and the language that you use is the tool you do it with.

"I just want to be happy."

"I don't need a lot of money."

"Good things come to those who wait."

"Everything happens for a reason."

Those are phrases we learn from others who are victims of F.U.D. They're both personally and financially **unsuccessful** and try to protect us from risk with their fears and experiences. When F.U.D. tells you that goals and success mean risk and failure, you tend to believe the warnings and stay where you are.

It's normal to **rationalize** that things happen outside your control when you don't know you can make these changes on purpose. It's also comforting to imagine things happen for the *right reasons.*

In reality, those feelings are another signal that change is desperately needed because we're not living the life we want. The next time you feel like your successes are influenced by outside forces, stop and remind yourself of this:

Everything happens for a reason, and the reason is me.

Step 1: Great Accomplishments

Step 2: Personal Identity

Step 3: Turn F.U.D. into Facts

Step 4: Turn Great Accomplishments into *Now* ideas.

Step 5: Change what you say to determine where you go

Step 6: Goal Design with Gap Analysis and RDOM2

Chapter 8 went into detail on designing our goals using Gap Analysis and RDOM2. I talked about how I created this system from successful IT projects, and how goals in our personal life work the same way. And you don't have to look further than the graphic, and basic steps below, to make this work for you.

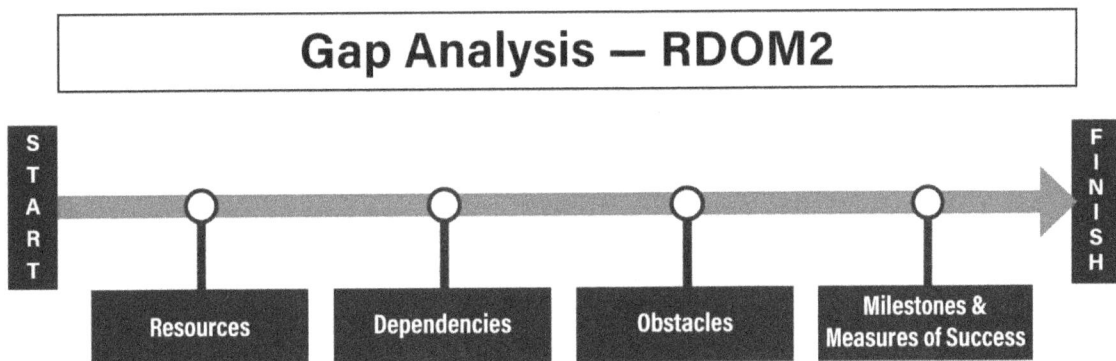

1. First, we define the Finish line of our goal in detail, which is our Great Accomplishment.

2. Next, we research, to find all the Proven Actions we need to achieve that.

3. Proven actions tell us the Resources we need, like time, money, or *other resources*. Other resources are anything that isn't time or money, like tools, skills, or help from someone else.

4. Then we organize our complete list of resources into the RDOM2 categories in the middle, known as The Gap, which does three things for us:

   a. Determine how and when we can get the resources we don't have now.

   b. Clarify proven actions, to make sure they're the right ones and no others are missing. That helps us adjust our resource list as we go, to make sure it's always correct for the actions we need to take.

   c. Find delays in our schedule, based on how and when we can get the resources we need to take our proven actions.

Everything we need in a goal design is a resource. Dependencies, like money, are also resources, and we need them first to be able to get other resources. Obstacles keep us from starting or finishing a part of our goal, and we need to think through the actions we design to see where and when those could affect us.

Milestones are how we prove we're making the progress we said we would. They show us when we've accomplished a step in our goal design, and Measures of Success are the proven measuring tools we trust.

As we're working through our proven actions, we want to review our design and ask ourselves some questions:

1. What other *Actions* does this design need?

2. What other *Resources* do I need?

3. What other *Dependencies* exist?

4. What other *Obstacles* are there, and **what could become one**?

Goal Design Is Like A Party: Creating a successful goal design is as easy as creating and managing your list for a party. That list is a design, and if you've ever made one to buy food and other items for a party, you've successfully managed a Gap Analysis using RDOM2.

- You visualized the Finish Line, which were all the items you needed for the party, and all the people you needed to help you.

- You compared those to your Starting Point, which were the people and things already available to you.

- You made your list based on the gap between what you needed and what you had.

The more skilled you become with Gap Analysis and RDOM2, the more time you save by being efficient with planning, designing, and taking actions.

Managing our time, money, and other resources affects our levels of success, and is another lesson we weren't taught as kids. That's why things felt so unclear in the past, and you won't realize how much time and effort you've wasted until you practice being efficient and purposeful now. Once that happens you won't be able to live the old way and knowing how and when to do the right things will start to feel like success by themselves.

That's how to create the best version of your life, and why I say you can start transforming yourself today.

Step 1: Great Accomplishments

Step 2: Personal Identity

Step 3: Turn F.U.D. into Facts

Step 4: Turn Great Accomplishments into *Now* ideas.

Step 5: Change what you say to determine where you go

Step 6: Goal Design with Gap Analysis and RDOM2

Step 7: Creating a Budget for Success

In Chapter 9, we talked about needing a Budget for Success. That's how to manage our resources in the most effective way. When we don't manage our time, money, and other resources, it's because we think we'll always be able to get more later. We won't, but without a goal design to show us the resources we need and the dependencies they have, we simply don't realize the successes we're giving up by wasting them.

We Can't Afford to Waste Time: Think about what happens when we waste time. Not only can we never get it back, but we limit the number of great accomplishments we can create. Wasting time now means we have to use time in the future to make up for what we didn't do when we should have.

We Can't Afford to Waste Money: When we spend money on things that don't help us achieve our goals, we have to delay taking actions in our goal design that cost money. We also have to do more work in the future to earn that money back, so we can take the actions we had to wait on.

That means we're wasting money twice, both today and tomorrow, and only getting one set of actions done. That makes our actions cost twice as much, and the number of goals we can achieve in a year becomes less than it should be.

An example I've seen all too often is when people buy a car or a home that costs so much, they don't have enough money left over each month to do anything else for themselves. The common idea is they expect to earn more later, without realizing the power they're taking away from themselves by spending that money now.

Remember the *Domino* and *Elimination Effects*. The choices we make now can cause us to make others in the future we normally wouldn't or take some away from us we'll never have access to.

We Can't Afford to Waste Other Resources: *Other Resources* simply means things that aren't time or money. Examples are help from other people, or tools we need for our goal. And just like time and money, we have to plan for and treat *Other Resources* with the same respect for their value. Otherwise, they may not be available when we're finally ready, or they might change their mind about helping us at all. That's the Elimination Effect.

Qualifying Questions for Resources in Your Budget for Success:

1. Does this information/person/tool help me?

2. In what way does it help me?

3. For how long will it help me?

Using a Budget for Success, to maximize our goal designs, is when the value of qualifying our resources becomes much clearer. It might seem obvious to say that someone or something is a resource to us, but we need to prove that with specific details to make sure it's our best choice.

When you ask yourself qualifying question 2, think of it as two parts:

➢ What *Problem* does this *Resource* solve for me?

➢ What new *Value* could this *Resource* create for me?

It's not enough to answer question 2 by saying "*a lot*" or "*in all the ways I need*," because that's not detailed enough to tell us the full story. Instead, you have to tell yourself clearly the problem it solves and any new value it creates.

To create bigger successes that happen at faster speeds, we need a budget for success to guide our goal designs every time. Otherwise, we're just hoping, wishing, and wondering about what we're doing and how things will turn out.

It's easier than you think to change your life, and with a little practice you'll automatically ask yourself these questions throughout the day:

1. Are my Resources supporting my Goal Designs and Great Accomplishments?

2. Does my Personal Identity represent *who I need to be,* to accomplish *what I want to do*?

3. Is F.U.D. keeping me from taking Proven Actions?

4. Am I still on schedule for creating success?

5. What needs to change *Now*?

Imagine how much bigger and faster your goals will become when you have clear answers to those every day.

Everything we want to accomplish needs clear answers, and when you have these tools and techniques on your side there's no such thing as failure. By focusing on building your *Three Pillars of Success* you'll develop the skills you need to succeed for the rest of your life.

It will be my greatest feeling of success when your fire reignites, and you feel Born to Succeed once again. Right now, it doesn't matter if you have a great accomplishment in mind, a goal design to support it, or any proven actions to take yet. The only thing you need is the confidence to tell yourself you can do anything you want starting today.

If you're a student, I want you to have the vision to design the right education and career, without believing the old lessons that say, "*go to school, get a good job, and get to safety.*"

As an Entrepreneur, I want you to realize that now is the time to change your business, by eliminating the Fears, Uncertainties, and Doubts that tell you "*it's too soon,*" "*wait to see what happens,*" or "*you've done enough for now.*"

And if you're in a career you don't love, I want you to have the courage to change course and make a plan for creating the life you most want. Life is too short to work for safety without success, and now is the time to decide *what* to change, and *when*. It's also time to remove the *barriers* and *speed limits* from your Personal Identity by asking yourself "*how do I know I can't make this change?*"

All goals take time, and I said many times we need proven skills and actions to succeed with our accomplishments. The key is identifying exactly the type of life we want, the type of person we need to become, and eliminating the fears that have always held us back.

For most of my life I was limited by the Fears, Uncertainties, and Doubts that were formed in my childhood. They told me I wasn't good enough, smart enough, or *deserving* of the life I saw others living. Then, because I couldn't "*see myself*" as "*that type of person,*" I never was, because *what you say determines where you go*.

Those feelings drove me to make poor choices in pursuit of money and safety, which is how I created the *Domino* and *Elimination Effects* that set me up for failure. I was 21 years old before I learned that I wasn't destined to struggle like my family had, but it took 25 more years to figure out who and what I really wanted to be.

However, *everything happens for a reason* when you don't know what you're doing, which in my experience is a *series of reasons* that add up to how we feel about ourselves. That feeling dictates the choices we feel able to make and is what created the life we're living right now.

But all that can change. We can stop that *Cycle of Failure,* to transform ourselves, and create a *Cycle of Success*. Starting today, we can design the life we want to live by telling ourselves this:

Change *is* coming, and today, it begins with me.